The Salvation Army
Farm Colonies

The Salvation Army Farm Colonies

Clark C. Spence

The University of Arizona Press
Tucson

About the Author

CLARK C. SPENCE is a western historian whose primary interest has been in the history of American mining. He is author of *British Investment and the American Frontier* and *Mining Engineers and the American West*. He is probably best known for *The Rainmakers*, which like his study of the Salvation Army farm colonies, was a product of his general interest in American history. The author has been a professor of history at the University of Illinois at Urbana-Champaign since 1963 and is a past president of the Western History Association.

To Wilma and Charlie

THE UNIVERSITY OF ARIZONA PRESS

Copyright © 1985
The Arizona Board of Regents
All Rights Reserved

Library of Congress Cataloging in Publication Data

Spence, Clark C.
   The Salvation Army farm colonies.

   Bibliography: p.
   Includes index.
   1. Christian communities—Salvation Army—History.
2. Fort Romie (Calif.)—History. 3. Fort Amity (Colo.)—
History. 4. Fort Herrick (Ohio)—History. I. Title.
BX9727.3.S64   1985   267'.15   85-8763

ISBN 0-8165-0897-6 (alk. paper)

Contents

Acknowledgments

MANY PEOPLE have contributed to this story of the Salvation Army farm colonies. I am grateful indeed to the respective staffs of the Bancroft Library, the Huntington Library, the British Museum, the Denver Public Library, the Houston Public Library, and the State Historical Society of Colorado. Without the broad general knowledge and the support of those at the Salvation Army Archives and Research Center in New York City this project would have been impossible. My thanks go to Tyrone B. Butler, Judith Johnson, and especially to Thomas Wilsted, who understands both historians and archives and who has helped me immeasurably.

I am grateful to the Salvation Army for inviting me as a participant to the Biennial Meeting of the Eastern Territory's Historical Commission in June 1984. It both pleasing and encouraging to know that modern Salvationists cherish their history and are concerned about its preservation, its accuracy, and its writing.

I also wish to thank several agencies for generous financial support of this study at various stages: the American Philosophical Society, the Department of History, and the Research Board, both of the University of Illinois.

C. S.

CHAPTER ONE

A Quiet Life
in the Country

How happy in his low degree,
How rich in humble poverty, is he,
Who leads a quiet country life,
Discharged of business, void of strife,
And from the griping scrivener free![1]

ON U.S. HIGHWAY 50, A FEW MILES west of the town of Holly in south-eastern Colorado, the modern traveler, if he looks closely, can see a marker placed by the Daughters of the American Revolution to designate one branch of the Old Santa Fe Trail. Nearby, a neat highway sign signals the existence of Amity, which consists of one residence and several buildings of a feed and grain company, drying equipment included. North of the road are the crumbling ruins of a few dwellings of an earlier era. Close by, lying on its top, is the rusting remains of a wrecked Chevrolet. To the south is the Santa Fe railroad line. All around are green fields, evidence of a thriving agriculture.

These tangible reminders are all that is left of what was at the turn of the century a prosperous settlement, the Salvation Army colony of Fort Amity, one of three such enterprises founded in the United States as experiments to relieve urban poverty by a subsidized back-to-the-land movement. One of the others, Fort Herrick in Ohio, was quickly turned into a haven for alcoholics. The third, Fort Romie in California's Salinas Valley, was the most successful. All were the products of the fertile brain of General William Booth, father and first leader of the Salvation Army, and of the organizational skills of his son-in-law, Frederick Booth-Tucker, commander of the Army in the United States.

None of these colonies is well-known, save by a few dedicated local historians. The handful of existing published descriptions are incomplete or are still colored by a good deal of misinformation. In January 1940, for example, when the Colorado Writers' Project did a piece on place names in *The Colorado Magazine*, it managed to include four glaring factual errors in a single brief paragraph about Fort Amity. Five years later, a badly mangled account of Fort Romie by a California author belittled the residents, made the whole undertaking sound like one big prayer meeting and noted that the colony "became famous as a perfect communal experiment" (which it did not and was not).[2]

The American Salvation Army colonies were not created in a vacuum. Colonization, that is, occupation of new lands or even old lands by more or less organized groups, is almost as old as mankind and has been undertaken in different times and in different parts of the world for a variety of reasons. The extension of suzerainty by establishing settlements goes back at least as far as the Greeks; the inviting of colonists from outside to strengthen a nation's hold on its own lands has long been a deliberate strategy, whether in the Russia of Catherine II or in the British Empire of George III. The particular approach of the Salvation Army had its antecedents in literally hundreds of farm colonies advocated by individuals, by charitable or religious societies and even city and national governments in all parts of the globe, generally with benevolent aims: to aid the needy, improve living conditions, reform criminals, or diminish the breakup of families.

A well-known example might be Frederiksoord, established in the depression that followed the Napoleonic Wars when a Dutch army general founded the Society of Beneficence to aid returning veterans. Begun in 1818, Frederiksoord was the first of several poor colonies in northern Holland where unemployed married men from the cities were trained on large farms preparatory to being settled on small freeholds of their own.[3] No less than Louis Napoleon Bonaparte had in 1844 published a pamphlet, *Extinction du Paupérisme*, in which he proposed state-subsidized agricultural settlements on unused French lands for urban workers idled by business failure or new technology.[4] The city of Paris early founded the nearby farm colony of La Chamelle. In Belgium a comparable enterprise was established near Wortel and another in 1825 at Merxplas, the latter primarily for tramps and beggars. Other agricultural work settlements cropped up in Switzerland, Saxony, and Holstein, with the most important coming in the 1880s at Wilhelmsdorf on the initiative of Pastor von Bodelschwingh and underwritten by both philanthropy and provincial government to bring together wasteland and waste-labor.[5]

Across the Channel, fire-eater Feargus O'Connor rallied his Chartist followers behind the idea of rural farmsteads for industrial workers and actually established several such settlements between 1846 and 1848.[6] O'Connor was one of the most radical but was not alone in denouncing rural depopulation, the evils of the industrial city, and in arguing that a numerous and prosperous peasantry was vital to Britain's national welfare. In the depressed 1880s, especially, considerable public support was thrown behind the "three acres and a cow" movement to stop the drift to the cities and improve living conditions of farm laborers on the land. At the same time, cheaper lands abroad, particularly within the empire, led to numerous experiments overseas. Lenient land policies in Canada, for example, encouraged colonization schemes by private companies and also by British landed aristocracy like Lady Gordon Cathcart, General Sir Francis de Winton and Baroness Burdett Coutts, all of whom underwrote colonies in Saskatchewan in the early eighties.[7]

By the same token, the German industrialist and philanthropist, Baron Maurice de Hirsch had planted a Jewish settlement in the same province in the middle of the same decade and was the acknowledged leader in supporting Jewish migration from eastern Europe. Through de Hirsch or through agencies like the Mansion House Committee of London or the Jewish Colonization Association, dozens of Jewish agricultural colonies were founded, especially after violent pogroms precipitated a heavy Russo-Jewish migration to the western world from 1881 to 1882, with organized settlements planted as far afield as Palestine, Argentina, Canada, and the western United States, replete with such colorful place names as Beer-Sheba, Kansas; Devil's Lake, North Dakota; and Cotopaxi, Colorado.[8]

These were all private efforts, although a government in Canada, for example, might be the indirect source of cheap land. But land was not enough where the urban needy were concerned. Free farms were available for homesteading in the United States after 1862 and in the Canadian West beginning in 1873. But to take advantage of such opportunity, especially in depression periods when back-to-the-land interest was highest, a poor family ideally required additional support for transport, implements, livestock, and living until a crop was harvested. Hence, invariably the supporters of colonization as a welfare measure sought to involve the official agencies of government.

During the sessions of the Forty-fifth Congress, in 1877 to 1878, for example, at a time when the nation still suffered from the depression which had commenced in 1873, at a time when the Grand Army of the Republic still sought benefits for veterans and when it was commonly believed that western agriculture was suffering little if at all, three bills were introduced by representatives of hard-hit industrial centers to provide federal aid for the urban unemployed to take up farms in the West. None passed, to be sure.[9] Not until the Great Depression that began in 1929 would Washington deign to play a direct role in agricultural resettlement on behalf of the public welfare. But reformers were quick to cite the few instances of the nineteenth century in which national funds had been applied to aid individual land utilization.

When seeking to invoke government support of his farm colonies, Frederick Booth-Tucker, commander of the American wing of the Salvation Army, liked to note the enlightened example of New Zealand, which in the mid−1880s began systematic efforts to settle the working classes as independent, self-supporting landowners. In response to severe depression, the Government Advances to Settlers Act of 1894 made available public funds to be reloaned to farm owners and real-estate holders at low rates of interest. At the same time, New Zealand inaugurated a policy of dividing large estates into small farms, to be settled with the use of these public loan monies. In addition, Booth-Tucker pointed to another New Zealand precedent: by 1899, forty state-sponsored Improved Farm Settlements had been established to give the unemployed work experience on roads, forests, and open lands.[10]

Nineteenth-century America had its own rich tradition of colonies of all kinds. Behind them, as behind most agricultural colonies everywhere, lay a set of fundamental concepts as old as antiquity—an almost proverbial faith in the superiority of farm life over any other. Historically, men described these beliefs in various ways. "To dwell upon the land and to eat the bread of toil is man's natural condition," said Cicero. "Those who are occupied with the cares of husbandry are freest from evil designs," wrote Cato. Thomas Jefferson insisted that "the small land holders are the most precious part of a state." "The first farmer was the first man," noted Emerson, "and all historic nobility rests on possession and use of the land." "The cultivation of the earth is the most important labor of man," argued Daniel Webster. "The farmers, therefore, are the founders of human civilization."[11]

Land and its tillage was the God-given fount of liberty, security, opportunity, and self-satisfaction. In the happy, healthy yeoman farmer and his family were personified all the admirable virtues: honesty, industry, sobriety, clean living, neighborliness, independence, a spirit of equality and fair play. Close communion with a beneficent nature somehow inevitably assured physical and moral well-being. These time-honored ideas came to fruition among intellectuals on both sides of the Atlantic in the eighteenth century, as such men as Rousseau, Crevecoeur, de Tocqueville, and Jefferson became their eloquent and effective spokesmen. To the most extreme, the Physiocrats, agriculture was the only source of economic value and even Adam Smith would agree that it was a primary and indispensable base. By the nineteenth century, the idea of the primacy and superiority of farm life and the set of values that went with it had been taken up by the masses and had become very much a part of political folklore and nationalist ideology. Even in the twentieth century, as the United States became predominantly urban, these values remained important. Only since the mid−1950s have scholars attempted to put into proper perspective these venerable rural values that Richard Hofstadter calls collectively the "agrarian myth," Leo Marx the "pastoral ideal," Marvin Meyers the "Old Republican idyll," and Henry Nash Smith the "myth of the garden."[12]

Self-sufficient farming invariably gave way to commercial agriculture and the Industrial Revolution flourished with all its implications in both the new world and the old. Like Britain, the United States was in a state of flux as the nineteenth century wore on and as it changed, the back-to-the-land movement gained a momentum it could not have had when the country was still overwhelmingly rural. Rapid industrialization and urbanization went hand in hand, with both positive and negative results. Cities grew feverishly at the expense of the countryside, as farm population declined in relative terms. To many of the newcomers flocking in—immigrants or farmers' sons and daughters—the city represented excitement, economic opportunity, upward mobility. It was "the cradle of progress." To others, cooped up in dingy boarding houses or in dank tenements located in vice-ridden, crime-infested unsanitary ghettos, the real city was something else. At least part of late nineteenth-century America watched with bewilderment as many of her best sons defected to the city and lamented that "all the agrarian virtues should have been sold so readily for a mess of pavement."[13]

Many invoked anew the myth of the superiority of the country. Pity the poor city dwellers, "utterly divorced from all the genial influences of nature," wrote Henry George, one of the best known of reformers, in 1883.

> The great mass of them never, from year's end to year's end, press foot upon mother earth, or pluck a wild flower, or hear the tinkle of brooks, the rustle of grain, or the murmur of leaves as the light breeze comes through the woods.[14]

Poets like Sam Walter Foss sang the glories of rural life and the hardship of the city.

> *But my boys they write from Boston, that for feet*
> > *that waded through*
> *The early fields of clover and the daisies and the dew,*
> *The stones are hard and cruel there on Boston's*
> > *biggest street*
> *And are pressed each day and hour by a horde of tired*
> > *tired feet.* [15]

In practice, most reformers—including the Salvation Army—by the mid–1890s sought to redeem the city in concrete ways. Evidencing a growing interest in poverty, as apart from simple pauperism, they began to look at the broader social questions. Social workers concerned with the disappearance of a sense of community in the urban environment would attempt to reestablish a more personal, informal neighborhood relationship through settlement house facilities and improvements. Some religious denominations followed the lead of the Catholics and the Salvationists by insisting that the church must adjust to the new setting and play a practical role in the redemption of the fallen city. A number of ministers began to preach and to act the Social Gospel: to examine the vital questions of the slum—vice, crime, labor conditions, or political corruption—and to do social work themselves, although middle-class American churches were often slow to adapt to the conditions caused by rapid urban and industrial growth. Some reformers, such as novelist William Dean Howells, saw the solution in more scientific city planning; designers such as landscape architect Frederick Law Olmstead helped inspire a movement for beautifying of cities. But it would be the progressive reformers of the early twentieth century, working at local, state, and national levels, who would fashion the most extensive actual improvement of the city climate of life.

Despite the ever-increasing flow of newcomers into the urban centers, the back-to-the-country movement was always there in the background, more obvious in time of depression than in prosperity. While much of the movement was theoretical, literary, or nostalgic, it had an impact on planned settlement as well as the individual. And in spite of all its individualism, or perhaps because of it, nineteenth-century America had a luxuriant tradition of utopian farm colonies. American optimism, confidence in social progress, cheap, available, fertile land and the absence of governmental limitations had encouraged numerous antebellum experiments by both religious and secular groups, ranging from Rappites, Zoarites, and the Amana Society to

Owenites, Fourierists, and the followers of Etienne Cabet. Later in the century, colonies were planted by Social Gospelites, socialists (both evolutionary and Christian), single-tax supporters of Henry George, and Nationalist disciples of Edward Bellamy. Many of these, especially the secular associations, believed that the only "practical" response to the ills of the new industrio-urban society was to withdraw into idyllic communities of their own.

In colonial New England, frontier towns had often been established by community action, but with a few notable exceptions the Trans-Mississippi West was settled by individuals or by groups of individuals loosely and temporarily organized for protection or companionship. Group migration and deliberate colonization were not unknown; and, indeed, the Mormons provide the example par excellence. But as has been pointed out, Mormon settlement was a blend of cooperative and business venture, with many original tasks handled jointly but with individual farming and private enterprise coming to the fore as an area matured. Yet because of the belief that Zion — the Kingdom of God — would be created on earth, Mormon colonization was in itself utopian. Commander Booth-Tucker was always impressed with the Mormons' success in resettling poor people, the more so when assured by the Latter Day Saints that church money advanced to settlers had always been recovered without the slightest difficulty. Like the commander, Latter-Day Saint leaders believed in the movement of families, rather than individuals. The family, said Booth-Tucker, ". . . roots the man to the land and the labor of the children is invaluable." As for farm settlement, he added,

> I value it most of all as an opportunity of making Soldiers for the Salvation Army. Look at the Mormons again: they have built up a powerful church simply by means of colonization, this is the basic policy in their social foundation.[16]

In some ways, Forts Romie and Amity were akin to the Mormon colonies, with a beneficent church organization providing financial support and ongoing guidance, but without the close religious cohesion of the Mormons. Salvationist leadership was always present and numerous colonists were indeed "Soldiers" in the Army, but other denominations were welcomed and no active church affiliation or attendance was required.

In some repects, too, the Salvation Army settlements resembled several Catholic efforts in Minnesota during the depression of 1873. There, beginning in 1876, Archbishop John Ireland of St. Paul, had opened five colonies on some 300,000 acres of railroad grant land, purchased at low price and passed on to urban Catholics, mainly Irish, at convenient low-interest rates. Ireland selected the land, organized a bureau to publicize it and chose a priest who knew something about farming to preside over each new colony. Still, these were not city down-and-outers; each participant needed a reserve of about $500 before beginning. These ventures led to the formation of the Irish Catholic Colonization Society of the United States, to carry on the same work in both Minnesota and Nebraska, again among those with some funds of their own.[17]

It is of note that the two major Salvation Army colonies in the United States were in California and Colorado, both states with formidable histories of colonization. In the century following 1850, California had more utopian settlements than any other state. Going back to at least 1869, Colorado produced a flurry of colonies of all kinds—utopian, cooperative and semi-cooperative—many of which failed but some of which developed into such permanent and prosperous centers as Greeley and Longmont.[18] But because of the uniqueness of the Army's approach, it is impossible to make valid comparisons. Romie and Amity were the only ones sponsored in a depression situation by a patron who provided start-up capital, organization, direction, and written contracts, and who promised not mere philanthropy but a business proposition. There was no utopianism here and only in the first few weeks was there any communal living. If the Army set down regulations, including a ban on alcohol, its paramount objective was to create a body of self-sufficing, land-owning farmers; and of course, as both General Booth and Commander Booth-Tucker would freely admit, it was also to swell the ranks of "Soldiers" in the Salvation Army, the ultimate objective. Basic to their religion was the concept that personal salvation was the only ultimate remedy for all human misery.

CHAPTER TWO

In Darkest England

*As the race from the Country to the City has been the cause of
much of the distress we have to battle with, we propose to find a
substantial part of our remedy by transferring those same
people back to the country, that is back again to the "Garden."*[1]

GENERAL WILLIAM BOOTH WAS a controversial figure in a nineteenth-
century England notable for its controversial figures. Booth had grown
up in poverty and knew firsthand the misery that attended urban life
with the coming of the Industrial Revolution. An ordained minister, he
early became the champion of the "bottom dog" and came fervently to
believe that his mission and that of the religious organization he
founded was to carry the word of God to the "unreached and the
unchurched," that is, the degraded poor whom other sects ignored.
Autocratic, narrow in outlook, antiscience and antiphilosophy in a
formal sense, Booth devoted his life to this cause even though his
increasing militancy made him the target of much ridicule and some
physical abuse. From the inception of the Salvation Army, Booth was
convinced that practical efforts to ameliorate the terrible living conditions of the downtrodden were essential to achieve the ultimate end.
". . . I must assert in the most unqualified way that it is primarily and
mainly for the sake of saving the soul that I seek the salvation of the
body," he explained.[2]

In 1861, Booth had left an orthodox Methodist pulpit to become an evangelistic preacher. By 1865, his calling had taken him into London's East End and some of the worst slums in England. There he organized his work under the name Christian Mission, but as his activities spread, in 1878 he changed the designation to the Salvation Army and subsequently developed a semimilitary framework under which to wage his war against the forces of Evil. Orders and regulations were drawn up in the fashion of the British army; posts became "corps"; standard uniforms were adopted; Booth himself became the General, with unquestioning obedience expected from other officers and from "soldiers" in the ranks. Under Booth's electrifying guidance, the Salvation Army took its religion to the poor—on street corners as well as indoors. It offered services that were simple and informal, eschewing sacraments and emphasizing joyous music, free prayer, and an open invitation to repentance.

But its militancy in public brought the Army more brickbats than bouquets. Middle-class critics sniped away from the press and a determined opposition condemned the Salvationists as fanatics whose approach was both crude and inflammatory. Many open-air meetings were disrupted by catcalls, open violence, or arrest for disturbing the peace. But Booth persisted; despite antagonism, the movement spread throughout the British Isles and some of the overt hostility began to wane.

It was the slums of such cities as London that remained Booth's first concern. There lived the "submerged tenth," most of England's three million poor, homeless, criminal, and vice-ridden, a mass equal to the population of Scotland. It was the surge of vast numbers of country folk into the city that had "been the cause of much of the distress we have to battle," Booth concluded; hence the solution was to reverse the flow. Late in 1890, in his provocative book, *In Darkest England and the Way Out*, its title capitalizing on Henry M. Stanley's recent work on Africa, the General set forth the rough outline of a set of proposals designed to uplift the poor and gradually to bring them back to the land, a scheme he called "a very simple one" with ramifications "for the whole world."[3]

Perhaps Booth had been influenced earlier by the passionate back-to-the-land efforts of Chartist Feargus O'Connor in the 1840s. In 1842, he had heard this "large 48-year-old Irishman with a rich baritone voice" lecture in Nottingham on the need to break up large estates and settle industrial families upon them. O'Connor had conducted a lively campaign by press and pamphlet and actually did manage to establish a number of land settlements before the bubble burst in 1848.[4] How much of this Booth may have followed is conjectural: certainly, he was not unaware of this vein of Chartist activity.

In Darkest England and the Way Out was a blueprint of the General's assessment of urban poverty and his ideas for relief. Booth had begun writing the book in 1888, but had bogged down after it was discovered that his wife, Catherine, was dying of cancer. At that point, the project was taken over and the writing completed by William T. Stead, a prolific author who had published an exposé of the white slave trade, and who would ultimately write a best-seller in America, *If Christ Came to Chicago* (1894), as well as biographies of both William Booth and his wife.[5]

After graphically describing "the darkness" and the "submerged tenth" and their abject and hopeless misery, Booth presented his visionary scheme to create a concentric system of "colonies," designed to "take people out of the abyss of poverty, or from its slippery brink and place them where poverty is almost unknown," as one sympathetic writer put it.[6] At the "very centre of the ocean of misery" was to be the "City Colony," comprised of a number of "Harbours of Refuge for all and any who have been shipwrecked in life, character, or circumstances." These "Harbours" might include cheap food centers, shelters, labor yards, industrial workshops, rescue homes for "lost" women, retreats for inebriates or discharged convicts and other agencies to provide immediate relief, temporary employment, and an opportunity to "commence at once a course of regeneration by moral and religious influences." Soon some of the uplifted would go on to permanent jobs, some would return to friends or family, and the rest, "tested as to their sincerity, industry, and honesty," would be passed along to the "Farm Colony."[7]

Even in England, Booth insisted, arable land was inefficiently used. "Hundreds of square miles of land" lay in "long ribbons on the side of each of our railways," he said. "These railway embankments constitute a vast estate, capable of growing fruit enough to supply all the jam that Crosse and Blackwell ever boiled." Every county had its vacant farms, and if Englishmen chose to emulate the intensive cultivation of the Swiss or the Chinese, the ordinary field could be made to double or even triple its production.[8]

Out in the country, on farms of from 500 to 1,000 acres, located on good transportation lines to London but away from the baleful influence of the village pub, Booth would resettle the graduates, as it were, of the "City Colony." The "Farm Colony" would be self-sustaining: its members would raise livestock, poultry, and rabbits and carry out spade husbandry under a superintendent who knew the intricacies of market gardening. Surplus produce would be sent to the Army's cheap food centers in the city, while conversely the Army's Household Salvage Brigade would gather goods from door-to-door in the city and send scraps to the country to be recycled. Thus kitchen fats would become axle grease and soap; rags and waste paper would become reconstituted paper, of which the Army itself used thirty tons a week; food scraps would fatten hogs, who in return would provide manure for the truck gardens. From the piggery would arise "a great bacon factory for curing"; sausages "would be produced literally by the mile."[9]

Women as well as men were to be resettled and could be expected actually to enjoy the lighter agricultural work. ". . . It will indeed be a change as from Tophet to the Garden of Eden when the poor lost girls on the streets of London exchange the pavements of Piccadilly for the strawberry beds of Essex or Kent," predicted Booth. The colony would have its public school, its library and reading room for self-improvement, and colonists would be expected to follow the Army's stricture against profanity and alcohol. Some who had proved themselves might be settled on three- to five-acre individual allotments, with a cottage, a cow, and the necessary tools to become self-supporting, paying a weekly fee to repay the cost of setting them up. "In this way our Farm Colony will throw off small Colonies all round it," Booth prophesied, as he indicated that others might also be invited to take part in a cooperative farm experiment modeled after E. T. Craig's Ralahine endeavor in Ireland. But it was clear that the farm colony was for most of its participants a transitory learning experience looking to the future. It was to be "a Working Man's Agricultural University, training people for the life which they would have to lead in the new countries they will go forth to colonize and possess." "After trial and training," the majority would go to the "Over-Sea Colony," where millions of cheap acres awaited Europe's surplus populations.[10] So ran the dream.

As early as 1886, Booth had been impressed by the vast expanses of Canada and had written of those magnificent prairies to his son: "I intend to do something in the way of emigration yet worth naming."[11] Thus the "third and final stage of the regenerative process" was settlement on cheap lands over the oceans, preferably within the British Empire, somewhere with a pleasant climate and a high demand for labor. Once land title was obtained, an advance group would survey, build shelters, break the soil, and plant the first crop before the main body of colonists arrived. Once established, their farms flourishing, the settlers would repay the Army for their passage, implements, and land expense and become freeholders, conducting their own businesses as small capitalists. The "reformation of character," and of livelihood was now complete.

To further this end, Booth proposed the creation of a Universal Emigration Bureau in London, with the Army to acquire its own vessel, "the Salvation Ship," to be "a perfect beehive of industry" as well as "a floating temple," manned completely—captain to crew—by ardent Salvationists. Transported colonists would work en route to the ultimate utopia, preparing and serving food, cleaning decks, loading and unloading cargo; perhaps even sewing, knitting, or making shoes as the craft plowed along.[12]

Booth likened his scheme to "A Grand Machine," superimposed on the city slums,

> . . . drawing up into its embrace the depraved and destitute of all classes; receiving thieves, harlots, paupers, drunkards, prodigals, all alike, on the simple conditions of their being willing to work and to conform to discipline. Drawing up these poor outcasts reforming them, and creating in them habits of industry, honesty, and truth; teaching them methods by which alike that perishes and that which endures to Everlasting Life can be won. Forwarding them from the City to the Country, and there continuing the process of regeneration, and then pouring them forth on to the virgin soils that await their coming in other lands, keeping hold of them with a strong government, and yet making them free men and women; and so laying the foundations, perchance, of another Empire to swell to vast proportion in later times. Why not?[13]

The publication of *In Darkest England* created a mild sensation. The militancy of the early Salvation Army had already drawn the criticism of other religious groups, and it is not surprising that the book evoked a small storm of argument. Its supporters believed the scheme to be simple, practical, and without blemish: it offered the poor an opportunity to help themselves; it mixed socialism, common sense, and the Ten Commandments; and certainly General Booth was eminently qualified to carry it into effect—his zeal, enthusiasm, devotion, and administrative abilities were all beyond question. On the other hand, an outspoken anti-Booth group called the book "pure sensationalism"; found the plan itself utopian and unrealistic, not to say simplistic; and challenged the assumption that the nonworking poor could be transformed into productive members of society. Those who thought "Field-Marshal Von Booth" too dictatorial and his discipline too rigid argued that his scheme would undermine the family and encourage a despotic socialism.[14] One rebuttal, *"In Darkest England": On the Wrong Track*, called the essence of Booth's proposal "a huge and fatal blunder." In a series of letters to *The Times*, Thomas Huxley labeled it "mere autocratic Socialism, masked by its theological exterior."[15] "If General Booth had not been born to be the commander of a peace-loving army, he ought to have become a promoter of companies," said another critic. "The *'East End Regeneration Co., Limited'* has been floated. *In Darkest*

England, supplemented by his public speeches, forms the prospectus."
Ministers such as Robert Eyton and Philip Dwyer dismantled the
scheme from the pulpit, calling it "A Rash investment,"; while others,
including supporters of the atheist Charles Bradlaugh, complained
that it would give Booth absolute power and that it was a plan for the
enrichment and expansion of the Salvation Army—charges that at
least some preachers took pains to rebut.[16]

Only parts of Booth's proposal ever went into formal operation.
Except in haphazard and incidental fashion, the integrated three-tier
colony apparatus never developed, although there is no doubt that *In
Darkest England* gave the first great impetus to the Salvation Army's
social work. In the city, the Army did create an elaborate structure of
agencies to aid the poor and the unfortunate, but without any systematic feeding of regenerates into farm colonies and eventually overseas
colonies. Almost immediately, however, in 1891, the army took its first
step and purchased an estate near Hadleigh in Essex, the citizens of
which were not much enchanted with the idea of a "colony of rascals" in
their midst. There, by 1910, the organization had invested some
£10,000 to establish a farm environment for the employment and
training of those willing to work, ex-convicts included. In an economic
sense, the Hadleigh venture did not pay its own way; nor did it create
small freeholders. But as it progressed, it came to be regarded by the
Army as a successful vindication of one aspect of Booth's farm colony
ideas. It did provide agricultural experience and guidance and many
Hadleigh "graduates" would be sent overseas, especially after 1905,
when the Army involved itself more deeply in fostering emigration,
although not to organized colonies abroad as General Booth had envisioned. Meanwhile, the General kept the vision alive in speeches
received with enthusiasm as far afield as Scandinavia, India, and
Australia.[17]

CHAPTER THREE

Organizing the American Colonies

In its minutest details that charter of the workingman's deliverance, that bridge of hope, that machinery of help, have been established, built, set in motion.[1]

PERHAPS THE MOST FERTILE GROUND for General Booth's seed was in America, that land of contrast, that land of progress and poverty, as Henry George phrased it. One of the most vivid and devastating pictures of New York slum life, *How the Other Half Lives*, was published by Jacob Riis in 1890, the same year as Ward McAllister's description of the idle rich, *Society as I Found It* and Booth's *In Darkest England*. Except for children and virtuous women, Riis showed only limited sympathy for the economic underdog but he gave a shocking indictment of ghetto conditions and argued that poverty existed as part of a broader social question, not because the poor were lazy, intemperate, or immoral, a view that would gain wider currency further into the decade.[2] Booth's book itself also made an impact in the United States for much the same reason. It popularized the idea that improved economic conditions were vital to the moral uplifting of the poor—the exact opposite of the Gospel of Wealth tradition which had dominated much of nineteenth century thought and which held, in effect, that poverty was the result of individual weakness or defect of character. Surely any man able and willing to work ought to be able to live decently. Young Richard Ely, of Johns Hopkins University, might not accept the theory and recommendations of *In Darkest England* without reservations, but he spoke for many of the bright, new social scientists when he welcomed the volume as "a trumpet blast calling men to action on behalf of the poorest and most degraded classes of modern society."[3] The example of the Salvation Army working among the down-and-outers, reminded socially conscious people that "they who touch the soul must minister to the body, as Jesus did."[4] There was concern, too, over the growth of Catholicism, whose parish leaders were also involved in day-by-day work among the urban poor. At the same time, growing antagonism between capital and labor worried many. Thus, by the 1890s, a number of Protestant groups in America were convinced of the need to do practical missionary activity in the city slums.

In short, a new definition of poverty was being formulated. Prior to the end of the century, what had interested reformers had been pauperism, not poverty. Until he was completely down-and-out, poverty was a man's own business, not society's. In 1891, when Richard Ely sought to determine the number of indigent in the country, he found such a scarcity of statistical information that it was almost impossible to compile reliable figures. But this would change. The new view was that the poor as well as the paupers were part of the problem. As redefined, the poor were inadequately fed, sheltered, and clothed. A man might work hard all year, yet not have enough to maintain his family decently. That meant that his underage children might have to take jobs, his wife do piecework at home or, as was common in poor neighborhoods, take in regular boarders. Under the new construction, poverty was not to be studied as an isolated phenomenon, but as part of the larger economic whole, since the causes of privation and destitution were usually beyond the individual's control.[15]

No doubt the changing view of poverty was hastened by the depression which started in 1893, devastated economies on both sides of the Atlantic, and swelled the ranks of the unemployed to epic proportions. Back-to-the-land talk was in the air, much of it linked with irrigation, which was regarded by some as the coming thing; already a few entrepreneurs were at work developing water networks for lands to be offered for cultivation.

By this time, the Salvation Army was well established on American shores. From a precarious beachhead in 1880, it made a substantial impact in the United States over the next decade and a half. It survived an open revolt in 1884, when the leader of its American arm sought to incorporate an Army independent of William Booth. Salvationists were often exposed to vituperation and even physical abuse or were arrested for parading, drumthumping or hallelujah-singing in the streets; but they endured these trials, expanded, and flourished. General Booth made his first trip to America in 1886 and after his return home installed his son, Ballington, as Commander under whose steady hands the Army in the United States grew in numbers and in prestige and came to be accepted grudgingly by the public. When the gaunt, hawk-nosed, white-bearded General made his second visit to North America in 1894 he could note the difference in attitude when, looking like an Old Testament prophet, he spoke fondly of his *In Darkest England* scheme to a crowd of 4,500 in New York's Carnegie Hall.[6]

The Army weathered a near schism in 1896, when in a period of deteriorating personal relations, the General recalled the popular Ballington Booth from his American post, an action followed by strong criticism and bitter protest meetings condemning this flagrant example of British tyranny. But a major split was averted and William Booth sent his second daughter, Emma, and her husband, Frederick St. George de Lautour Booth-Tucker to take command and to heal the breach in early 1896. It was an excellent choice. Frederick Booth-Tucker has been described by his latest biographer as "William Booth's First Gentleman." The son of a British civil servant, he had been born in India, educated at Cheltenham College and had himself returned to Bengal in the civil service in 1876. Six years later, when he resigned his job and joined the Salvation Army, his father cut him out of his will and his life. It was Tucker who led the Salvation Army invasion of India in 1882. A gifted linguist and an intrepid missionary, he adopted local dress and moved to native quarters to preach to Indians in their own tongue. After the death of his first wife, while on a visit to England, he met and wed Emma, and like other men who married into the Booth family, he adopted the hyphenated surname, though to his father-in-law he always remained "Fritz." The couple returned to India until 1891 when Emma's poor health prompted a transfer to London where Booth-Tucker took charge of the Army's work outside the United Kingdom. Thus, when tapped in 1896 after the Ballington Booth crisis, both of the Booth-Tuckers had considerable practical experience behind them.[7]

When they arrived in New York, Emma was thiry-six, a "fine figure," tall, graceful, and an excellent and moving speaker. A born conciliator, she was, as someone called her, a "feminine spiritual Bismarck." Seven years older, her husband was a striking man, lean and lank of frame, with full mustache and hair worn longer than most of his contemporaries. A man of elegance and breeding, albeit described as a "stiff, cold invigorating wind," he was nonetheless a mixer and a dynamo of activity who appealed to a wide range of Americans.[8] He came to know influential political and economic leaders, including Mark Hanna and Theodore Roosevelt; he wrote incessantly for the press and popular magazines; through his countless lectures he became known the length of the land; and despite his background and his exalted rank he had that human touch that enabled him to don a

cowboy hat and become one of his people in the West or to pose
rustically for an artist as "The Man Behind the Plow."

In their American assignment, the Booth-Tuckers were coequal.
They were "Joint Territorial Commanders" of the Army, but Frederick would be known as the "Commander" and Emma as the "Consul."
As the two traveled about the United States in 1896 and 1897, they
began to see the potential for parts of the General's *In Darkest England*
vision, especially of moving the city unemployed to the open spaces of
the West. The worst of the depression was over and the economy was
righting itself but the urban poor were as obvious as ever. Soon the
Booth-Tuckers were channeling much of their energy into the farm
colony movement adapted to the western American scene.[9]

By early 1897, the San Francisco edition of the Salvation Army
organ, *The War Cry*, was beginning to reflect the growing enthusiasm of
American Army leaders for a colonization plan. Already the Army had
opened the Golden Gate Farm near Pacheco in Contra Costa County,
California, as a kind of half-way house for discharged prisoners—a
limited operation accommodating sixteen men at a time before it closed
early in 1898. The Salvation Army also ran the Cotati Wood Camp,
north of Petaluma, as a work haven for sixty-three men.[10] But neither
of these were colonies as such; rather they were social agencies of
transition.

Yet colonization was in the air. In January 1897 it was noted that
350 acres of farmland near Seattle had been willed to the Army and
that other possibilities were in the offing. One woman had offered
1,000 acres to be used for the rehabilitation of ex-convicts; elsewhere, a
possible 25,000 acres had been mentioned as a settlement site; another
person was confident that when the time came she would be able to help
secure a grant of 100,000 acres "for the foundation of the Army's
Western Colony," a prospect of a "modern Canaan below" which sent
at least one editor into rhapsody.[11]

When the Salvation Army in January issued its "Grand Call to
Arms," its "Plan of Campaign for 1897," it included in its aspirations
the "Capture of 75,000 Souls," the addition of 1,000 brass bandsmen,
five hospitals, a dozen "nursing battalions," rescue homes for 300 more
fallen women, and farm colonies for 100 families. That this was serious
business was indicated a few months later when Booth-Tucker appeared in San Francisco to outline a colonization plan to the Chamber
of Commerce. A seeker of money, but also a realist, he criticized the
idea that even half a million dollars could eradicate urban poverty:
colonization was not a panacea for the poor, he contended; its purpose
was to "build a bridge over which they might pass." Recalling the
famous "Pingree Potato Patches," the vacant-lot gardens organized by
the Mayor of Detroit to aid the unemployed to help themselves in the

dark years following the 1893 depression, Booth-Tucker advocated an application of the same principle on a more formal scale, using five-acre family plots in colonies of from 100 to 1,000 acres on which to settle out-of-work poor "as peasant proprietors."[12] Eventually, the Commander envisioned large settlements of 100,000 acres or more, established as business propositions with the basic aim of restoring "the forgotten art of homiculture." The movement of three million urban dwellers back to the soil would greatly enhance land values, and tax consumers would become tax producers. Two hundred families could colonize 1,000 acres, he calculated. Twenty single men would pave the way by preparing twenty plots, these to be taken up by twenty families, who in turn would break ground for the next fifty families. From proceeds of the sale of butter, milk, or other farm products or from occasional work on neighboring farms, colonists would gradually repay the Army for its outlay at a weekly rate. Land and willing settlers were available, said Booth-Tucker. Only capital was lacking: hence the Commander's appearance before the business community of San Francisco—to raise $25,000 to begin the first settlements.[13]

At Booth-Tucker's request, the Chamber of Commerce established a Committee of Fifteen and commenced a publicity campaign and a drive for funds. Booth-Tucker brought in Major Wallace W. Winchell from the Cotati wood camp to help work out details. A man of great ingenuity, Winchell had earlier made headlines in Chicago with his hand bill "subpoenas" in the highly publicized case of "the Salvation Army, plaintiff, vs. Satan; alias the 'Devil;' alias the 'Serpent'. . . ."[14] Winchell honed the rough edges off the colonization plan and helped give it form. He presented examples from the Army's experience in England, India, and Australia to prove that city folks could prosper and be happy in a farm setting. Good soil located near water and markets was vital, he noted, as he sketched out the role of the Army in the proposed endeavor. Each family would be allocated five acres; at the same time, the Army would reserve a core of forty for itself—thirty for grazing purposes and ten for a townsite. Here would be located headquarters and the residence of the "governor," the Salvation Army officer who would serve as superintendent of the colony. Here also would live an accountant responsible to New York or San Francisco. And here would be established all the trappings of civilized town life: bank, store, school, blacksmith, shop, dairy, barber shop, public hall, and clubroom.[15]

Both Winchell and Booth-Tucker believed $25,000 was a minimal beginning figure for settling fifty families. They calculated a total of $500 each with an estimated $200 for land, $150 for a cottage, and $150 for stock and improvements. Originally Winchell had thought in terms of a communal incubator to provide each family with 100 to 150 chicks, which would eventually produce from four to six dozen eggs daily and "support the man independent of the soil." Originally he believed that one or two pigs would "in the course of a year produce thirty or forty hogs" and enable the colonist to realize an additional $200 to $700 annually. But soon both Winchell and Booth-Tucker were talking of a cow, a pig, and thirty to forty chickens per family. They also discussed a weekly rental of one dollar, half to go for interest and half for repayment of capital. Such payments could be assured from pro- duce, by employing colonists in the settlement, by locating near large ranches where jobs were available, or even by a man's retaining his job in a city momentarily, while settling his family on the land.[16]

As the Army's plans were publicized, it was offered a selection of lands in California, ranging from property of the Cremelita Vineyard Company near Reedley to a portion of old General Bidwell's ranch near Chico. When sugar magnate Claus Spreckels proffered 700 acres of the Sobrante Ranch in the Salinas Valley at $60 an acre for arable and $25 for timber, Winchell and three members of the San Francisco Committee of Fifteen, including former mayor, L. R. Ellert, visited the property and were impressed—despite a four-horse runaway which left one animal dead in a barbed wired fence and plunged their wagon into the river.[17]

Meanwhile, under Ellert's chairmanship, the Committee of Fifteen set out to raise $10,000 as a gift for the colony project. Spreckels pledged his support and soon the committee expanded to thirty and sought to augment its outright donation by finding men of means to subscribe or underwrite by loans.[18]

With a special car at his disposal by the Santa Fe Railroad, Booth-Tucker now stepped up the search for a suitable site and at the same time intensified the publicity on the project. One point that he reiter- ated was the suitability of the Salvation Army for colonizing the poor. The Army had a reputation for honesty; it had both the numbers and organization to supervise masses; and its personnel were skilled in dealing with rascals as well as the poor. Moreover, its history of self- sacrifice and devotion inspired confidence in those it sought to lead. With 2,300 officers in charge of 730 American posts, the Salvation Army needed no introduction to the working man, said Booth-Tucker. "The uniform of its officer is his or her passport to every heart and home, to the lowest dives and saloons, to the cottage and the attic."[19]

The Commander noted that colonists would require careful selec- tion and training and that the Army was already organizing working men's lectures on agricultural subjects and proposing vacant lot gar- dens. It was now proposing small farms on city perimeters "where a further system of rough-and-ready preparation can be gone through."

By careful screening of colonists, breakdowns could be kept at a minimum. But, said Booth-Tucker, there was no dearth of potential settlers, no lack of land or water. The one essential which was missing was capital. Yet investment opportunities were limited: much capital was idle. The Army's plan for handling the unemployed, said the Commander was,

> ...in brief, to place Waste Labor on Waste Land by means of Waste Capital; thus combining this Trinity of Waste, the separation of which means the destruction of each, the cooperation of which means the prosperity of all.[20]

Like General Booth, he emphasized the importance of colonization to the Army's concept of social regeneration, arguing at the same time that a yeomanry was the nation's pride and strength: "The divorce of the small landed proprietor from the soil is the root cause of the depressed state of agriculture; and, until the balance of population can be restored from the city to the country, permanent prosperity on a national basis seems to me well-nigh an impossibility."[21]

Human needs and dignity should be paramount, he argued:

> Time was when a man was thought to be worth more than a sheep: now he is valued at less than a California ground-squirrel; inasmuch as we can neither poison him, eat him, nor sell his skin! This cannot be good economy, philosophy, statemanship, or Christianity. Something must be wrong somewhere.[22]

Meanwhile, Booth-Tucker had made the decision as to location of the first colony. Although Claus Spreckels had pledged a donation of $1,000, his property was passed over in favor of that of a neighbor, Charles T. Romie. Born in Germany, Romie had migrated to the United States in 1840. He was said to have begun his career in California as a vaquero, but by 1900 he would identify himself simply as "Capitalist." In the banking business he had taken over lands of Mission Soledad, lost by Benito Sobrenes, part of which he now passed on the the Salvation Army.[23] Romie's land was $10 an acre less than Spreckels', his terms more liberal.[24] Located a few miles from Soledad and the Southern Pacific Railroad line, with the Gabilan hills to the east and the Santa Lucia Mountains on the west, the old Sobrenes ranch had been visited by Booth-Tucker, Winchell, and several others at a time when only $4,000 in loan money was definite. They tramped over the light, loamy but rich soil; toured the crumbling Mission; spent the night at the Paraiso Hot Spring Hotel where they discussed the colony until late; then made the "hot dusty trail" back to the station by wagon, according to one who was there.[25]

The decision made, Booth-Tucker resumed his public relations work and announced that not one, but two colonies would be established. The president and vice president of the United States, he said, "have listened with interest to and have expressed sympathy in our plans." Land propositions had been received from twenty-three states and twelve railroad companies and a number of large landowners and irrigation concerns had given their endorsement.[26]

In August, traveling in the Santa Fe's private car, the Commander had examined lands in Colorado and New Mexico "suitable for his rescue colony." A bit later, he met in Denver with Governor Alva Adams, who presided over a large public meeting, at which Booth-Tucker described his back-to-the-soil plan, carefully reminding his audience of the heritage of earlier colonies at Greeley and Colorado Springs. Well-received, the Commander climbed back into his private car and headed east tothe Sixth National Irrigation Congress meeting in Lincoln, Nebraska, carefully routing himself through the Arkansas Valley, where attractive irrigated land was about to be opened. At Lincoln, after Emma Booth-Tucker had explained the colonization plan, the Congress by resolution lauded this "grand, noble, and patriotic work" and urged its support by "every citizen of our country."[27]

By the end of November, the Booth-Tuckers were in New York for the Salvation Army's massive five-day congress, which made "Back to the Land" its battle cry. At the final event on November 30—a "red letter night"—in "stirring speech and appeal," the Commander explained his ideas of colonization as a "national remedy" for the problem of poverty. Following a colorful procession of costumed Salvationists from all over the world, and the playing of a brass band and songs by the "Salvationist troupe of colored jubilee singers from Kentucky," Booth-Tucker announced that the Army would settle "several thousand acres of fertile land in the Arkansas Valley," which he erroneously placed in "western Colorado." This would be part of "...a chain of colonies which shall girdle the continent with help and hope, and shall form stepping stones from the dismal abyss of poverty to the happy homes of prosperity." As an added attraction, Booth-Tucker read letters expressing great interest from a number of public figures, including President William McKinley, Abram Hewitt, John Wanamaker, Francis E. Willard, and Alva Adams, who by prearrangement wired from Denver: "Accept my sympathy and confidence in your colonization scheme. Every industrious family planted on Colorado soil is a family made independent."[28]

The Commander asked the standing-room-only crowd at Carnegie Hall for loans, not necessarily gifts, repayable in ten years at five percent interest, in order to create a fund of $100,000 to place 200 families on 2,000 irrigated acres. At the end of the meeting, after pledge cards had been collected, it was announced that several persons had pledged $1,000 each, one $5,000, and that a total of nearly $30,000 had been raised.[29]

Soon Booth-Tucker was in Chicago, making arrangements for another large gathering, at which colonization would be the focal point. Ideally, he noted, with $50 million, three million paupers could be resettled. His appeal to a capacity crowd at the Central Music Hall raised $10,000 "within a few minutes" and indicated to the Commander that he had public support. By New Year's Day, he was convinced that he had adequate financing to proceed.[30]

Already, Booth-Tucker had signed a contract for 640 acres in the Arkansas Valley, six miles west of Holly, Colorado, only eight miles from the Kansas line. When the Commander had visited the site in the late summer, he had been accompanied by Colonel Thomas Holland, the Salvation Army officer who soon came to be regarded as the on-the-scene driving force of the colonies. Holland was said to have been "born on a sunshiny day, and has never got over the fact." From the day he was converted as a teenager in Liverpool, he had followed a career in the Army: village adjutant in the British Southern Division; drummer in the home corps; in charge of forty-two corps in Birmingham and Leicester; supervisor of children's work in London; field secretary and then chief secretary in Canada; supervisor of settlement of Armenian immigrants in the United States. Noted for his "no dilly-dallying" ways, Holland was considered by the Salvation Army "as the pushing, indefatigable pioneer of the Social and Colonization work in this country."[31]

Both Holland and Booth-Tucker had been impressed with the small-acreage melon-growing around Rocky Ford, where small landholders had been successful in market production. If Colorado could not absorb all the melons available, which was unlikely, a good eastern market also existed. Since watermelons and cantaloupes gave a good return on labor, Holland believed they were "destined to be an important factor in our proposed colony." Moreover, the land to the east of Rocky Ford came highly recommended. With water available from a huge new irrigation project, the region promised to become "a veritable garden of Eden" and the climate "appears to be as near to the ideal as one could desire." Although certain that Santa Fe Railroad officials, "good friends of the Army, would see that we had a good selection of land," Booth-Tucker nonetheless called in outside experts before he closed the deal.[32]

Thus by the end of 1897, funds had been raised and the sites selected for two western colonies. The soundings were good, the publicity positive. The *New York Sun* ran an article on "The Poor Man's Paradise," in which it noted that such hard-headed businessmen as

James Davis, general industrial commissioner for the Santa Fe, normally were skeptical of colony settlements—they "generally have no
money and no backing"—but were enthusiastic about the Salvation
Army plans.[33] Some westerners, former Mayor Platt Rogers of Denver
among them, originally questioned the wisdom of settling "an undesirable class of citizens," but changed their minds when convinced that the
Army would brook no nonsense and would quickly eliminate the
drones. "Tramp or pauper colonies . . . would be a dead weight,"
insisted the editor of the Denver *Republican*, who admitted that poverty
and bad character were not necessarily corollary partners. Careful
selection of settlers was the key. Certainly the valley between Pueblo
and the Kansas line could absorb 50,000 new people without overcrowding.[34]

Even after arrangements had been completed in California and
Colorado, other Salvationists were keeping their eyes open for additional sites. Early in 1898, Captain John Milsaps, the first Salvation
Army officer recruited and commisssioned in California, was touring
Arizona with "cornet and guitar, bass drum and stereoptican equipment" on a dual mission designed to save souls and to consider possible
colony sites. Well known on the Pacific Coast for his "blood-and-fire
style" and his "wide-awake hallelujah knee-drill," Milsaps met with a
real estate agent in Phoenix to discuss a proposition from the Estrella
Irrigation and Fruit Company. At Tucson, he had several discussions
about the colonization project with L. C. Hughs, former governor and
subsequently editor of the *Arizona Star*; and he met with Frank
Hereford, who was trying to sell the Army some land sixty miles south
of Tucson.[35] Nothing came from these negotiations. When the Army
added one more colony, it would be located in Ohio, and would seem to
have been more the result of chance than from any concerted campaign by officers to seek out a specific area.

In the spring of 1898, when the new California and Colorado
settlements were prospering with a good deal of fanfare, two Ohio
businessmen made land available for another colony near the boyhood
home of James A. Garfield, at Mentor, a few miles from Cleveland.
Myron T. Herrick, prominent banker and subsequently twice ambassador to France, and his brother-in-law, James Parmalee, in May offered Booth-Tucker 288 acres at a price the Commander thought "was
rather high." Herrick offered to reconsider and to let the Army "have a
rock bottom figure." He also agreed to lend the Army $5,000 at four
percent interest and to take back the property if at any time the Army
no longer wished to retain it.[36] Thus a deal was struck for the site of
what would become Fort Herrick, a brief experiment in colonization
that would soon deviate from the original plan.

CHAPTER FOUR

Fort Romie, California

But the latest is the Commander's Colonization Scheme;
If others were the milk, this would surely be the cream;
From the crowded cities they'd be drafted to the land,
For when God put man in Eden, this was what His heart
*   had planned.*[1]

THE ARMY ANNOUNCED EARLY IN 1898 that the first contingent of colonists had left Oakland for Soledad, California, where they would make their homes in the first of the chain of farm colonies with which Commander Booth-Tucker would eventually encircle the continent.[2] Actually, some three months earlier, the Army had let it be known that it was marshalling the first body of settlers for the California colony. More than three hundred had signed up, of whom more than eighty percent had "more or less experience in farming." Soon Booth-Tucker could inform a New York audience that "all the selected families were able-bodied agriculturalists" who for three months had undergone weekly instruction from a number of experts, including Salvationist Elizabeth McLean, a graduate of the University of California College of Agriculture and daughter of the Alameda County health officer, as well as Meyer E. Jaffa of the California Experiment Station and Eugene Hilgard, the pioneer scientist largely responsible for developing the University of California agricultural program. Hilgard also analyzed soil samples and would give help in other ways, among them "championing the sugar beet colony enterprise."[3]

"The sugar beet colony enterprise" was in part a function of location and the expectation that beets would from the first be an important cash crop. Situated 150 miles south and east of San Francisco "in the beautiful valley of the Salinas River," as Booth-Tucker called it, the site was four miles from Soledad and the Southern Pacific rail line, within easy range of Claus Spreckels' beet sugar factory at Watsonville and even closer to his soon-to-be-opened Salinas refinery—the largest in the world under one roof. Between these two plants, Spreckels had promised to buy all the beets that could be grown on the colony.[4]

The original site consisted of 519.03 acres of the old Mission Soledad Rancho, acquired from Charles Romie at a price of $25,951.50 at first under a temporary leasing arrangement, then in 1899 by outright purchase, with Romie holding a first mortgage on the property of $19,058.08 until more permanent financing was accomplished in 1901.[5]

On October 6, 1897, the first group of settlers left the Bay Area for Soledad, with a huge sign on their big four-horse farm wagon, "Ho! For Salvation Army Colony," and spare horses trailing in the rear. Lieutenant Tinsley of the Cotati Wood Camp was in charge, perched with half a dozen others atop a load of new and used farm implements in the vehicle. Two days later, another Salvation Army officer took a second load of machinery to the colony site, which was already being referred to as Fort Romie. As usual, the Army organized briskly and efficiently: Sergeant-Major Brown was in charge of home-building; Staff-Captain William Wood supervised overall work at the colony, while Major Wallace Winchell served as general coordinator and trouble-shooter.[6]

Charles W. Haskell of San Francisco had been hired to survey the land into tracts, and breaking the soil commenced less than forty-eight hours after the vanguard of settlers arrived. Such haste was based on the theory that crops were of prime importance and that houses could be built later on plowed land if necessary.[7]

Meanwhile, to save freight costs, the Salvation Army continued its supply runs by wagon to San Francisco and Oakland and the number of colonists grew, despite the fact that financing was not yet completely solidified. F. A. Hihn of the Committee of Fifteen and a lumberman helped acquire building materials at reduced cost and collected $1,000 from Santa Cruz residents; Harris Weinstock solicited $800 from Sacramentans, while other raised lesser amounts—enough to buy eight horses, two gang plows and other equipment. Hihn was also one of those urging the purchase of 8,000 additional acres for the Fort Romie experiment, a move that was never completed. Officers such as John

Milsaps canvassed an audience of about seventy-five at Watsonville for funds and also took the occasion to make "a long, strong pull for souls." An effort was also later made to get $1,000 in Monterey County funds, a proposal that was rejected, much to the satisfaction of *The Pacific Rural Press* editor. But by early December, it was reported that $5,000 had been subscribed and the Army was fully publicizing the "Lessons from California" already being learned at "The Salvation Army's Workingman's Paradise" nestled at the foot of the Santa Lucia mountain range.[8]

Commander Booth-Tucker stepped up the campaign with a series of orientation and fund-raising meetings in early 1898. On New Year's Day, with San Francisco Mayor James D. Phelan presiding, Booth-Tucker discussed colonization before a large group "and the audience of 3,000 persons was ablaze with regard for him," reported *Harbor Lights*, an Army publication in New York. He also addressed a captive audience of 1,000 at San Quentin Prison, and the next night at San Francisco's Golden Gate Hall, with Rabbi Jacob Voorsanger at the rostrum, he formally launched the colony drive. Voorsanger called for "prayer and hard cash" for the Soledad settlement, beginning with a ten-dollar donation of his own. Sixteen colonists were present to describe what had already been accomplished; a large painting of the colony was on display, as was the model of a ten-acre farm. It was there that the Commander, among others, made a fervent appeal for funds and named the colony Fort Romie after the former owner of the land, "who has proved himself such a good friend of the enterprise."[9]

On the following day, January 5, Booth-Tucker and a small entourage traveled to Fort Romie for formal opening ceremonies. Because of inadequate transportation several of the party had to walk the last five or six miles and one of them "gave out on the road."[10] At the time, there were thirty colonists on the scene, representing ten families, many members of which were to follow in a few days. Thirty cottages were up or under construction, plus the frame of a store. Until the houses were finished, the settlers ate communally (as they had done on Thanksgiving Day, when Charles Romie sent them a dozen chickens, 197 pounds of pork and two gallons of cranberries). The colonists owned nine horses of their own, the Army had provided seventeen more, and an additional nineteen had been borrowed from Romie. Booth-Tucker left the scene glowing with optimism that scarcely dampened even when it was discovered that Major Winchell had left behind the free railroad passes, and the party, with difficulty, had to find enough cash for the return to San Francisco.[11]

One of the group had been Manuel Valencia, a Bay area artist and photographer and illustrator for the Pacific edition of *The War Cry*. Valencia's pictures of colonies and colony scenes appeared also in San

Francisco newspapers. Readers of the *Examiner* or the Salinas press found complimentary descriptions of the "high-spirited, earnest, steady people" beginning new lives at Fort Romie. "Never seen such workers in my life," a local citizen is supposed to have said. John Milsaps of *The War Cry* directed West Coast publicity, loaned photographs, and countered the few wisps of negative comment which appeared. The editor and at least one outspoken reader of *The Pacific Rural Press* were especially critical. As they saw it, the scheme was "impracticable" and "based on the absurd notion that any sort of a man is good enough for a farmer."[12]

Who were these original colonists? A reporter for the Salinas *Index* who visited the settlement on a quiet April Sunday described them as optimistic city dwellers enjoying a rebirth in the country and pleased indeed with their treatment by the Salvation Army. According to *The War Cry*, the colony included three Salvationist families, five Methodists, one Baptist, one Catholic and the others of no particular religious preference. It was made clear that while the Salvation Army did hold three religious meetings each Sabbath and three during the week, settlers were free to follow (or not follow) their own practices. Colonists were confident and enthusiastic. One named Pascoe remarked that "he had found his Klondike. . . ." Three—McCurdy, Nils Hamrens, and Frank O. Lindstrand—had all been street railway employees in San Francisco and vowed not to go back even if guaranteed five dollars a day for the rest of their lives. G. A. Apringer had been at sea for many years. According to Booth-Tucker, the eleven original settlers had represented four different nationalities, born in ten different states or countries.[13]

With each colonist, the Army, through its Commander, entered into a formal agreement, whereby the colonist agreed to rent a specified acreage, with buildings, at a stipulated annual fee, payable in equal monthly installments, with an option to purchase if he met the requirements, including payment of rent and obligations for food, clothing, farm equipment or other goods advanced by the manager of the colony. He agreed to pay in cash or in labor, as the Army might designate, and he committed himself to take irrigation water from the colony during the ten-year lease period and after the purchase option was exercised at prescribed rates ($1.50 an acre in winter months and $2 an acre in the summer). On behalf of the colony, Booth-Tucker was empowered to act as agent in disposing of crops, with the right to retain up to one-half the entire proceeds to cover arrears of rent or loan payment. And "realizing that sobriety, industry, and faithfulness to the interests and welfare of the Colony are essential parts of this contract," the individual colonist agreed to conform to these qualities. If he appeared drunk or disorderly, he might be ousted with forfeiture of his claims, but with compensation for standing crops and other property rights as set by an arbitration committee. At the end of ten years, his purchase completed, he was promised a good title to his land, while he, on his part, agreed that he would ". . . not bargain, sell, barter or trade upon said land, any intoxicating liquors, or otherwise dispose of, as beverages, any intoxicants at any place upon said premises . . . or permit the selling of the same or any illegal traffic or any act or acts prohibited by law. . . ." Should the colonist fail to live up to these restrictions, then the colony had the right to "re-enter and take possession of said premises."[14]

There is no evidence of any great complaint of these terms by the settlers, although a few years later some questioned how strict enforcement should be of the no-alcohol clause. Perhaps this was what the editor of the *San Jose Herald* had in mind when he complained that the contracts left the colonists "in a state of practical serfdom. . . . They virtually abdicate not only their legal rights but their manhood to a considerable extent."[15]

In the 1890s the Army printed up application forms for prospective colonists, noting that the filling out of the form in no way obligated the applicant. At the same time, it printed a standard recommendation form with nine questions to be answered by those named as references. Among the queries were: "Is he industrious?" "Does he keep his situations?" "Is he addicted to the use of intoxicating liquors?" "Do you think he will settle happily in the country?" Questions on the use of liquor and on industriousness were repeated as they applied to the applicant's wife.[16] It is not clear that such recommendation forms were widely used but presumably they were an integral part of the selection process.

Also printed in the 1890s were detailed weekly report forms, to be signed by the colony superintendent and his assistant. These listed the number of families, men, women, and children; the number of temporary employees; the number of acres under cultivation, with breakdown by crop. They provided for a weekly count of horses, cows, pigs, and poultry and gave an accounting of income from farm rent, crops, and livestock. They provided for entry of all expenditures for wages, seed, lumber, and implements; noted what irrigation had been done for the week and asked the question, "What is the spiritual condition of the Colonists?"[17] Whether such forms were actually utilized is debatable. Probably not, although existing financial records of the colonies show a remarkably detailed day-by-day system of entries.

In any event, the colony expanded and seemed to progress. An ardent Salvation Army worker and former teacher, Mary Johnson, came down from Oakland to take charge of the new school. In late March 1898, according to Major Winchell, there were sixteen families, about eighty people, living at Fort Romie. Professor Jaffa from Berkeley spent several days there conducting a Farmers' Institute in March and again in April. Claus Spreckels reiterated his offer to buy all sugar beets grown, a crop estimated to be worth $15,000 even before it was produced. Charles Romie donated 2,000 eucalyptus trees, which along with cypress and other kinds, would be planted when irrigation commenced. And by mid-April, the colony had three new infants, including Lawrence Romie Tucker Winchell, son of Wallace Winchell, the "Colony dad." Of the new native, *Harbor Lights* could note with enthusiasm, "We expect when he is of age there will be hundreds of similar Colonies carrying hundreds of thousands of poor people from the cities into happy rural homes." Winchell was also in charge of the new United States post office, named Romie, because the government had refused to sanction "Fort Romie" on the grounds that Romie was no military establishment.[18].

The most pressing need was for completion of an irrigation system. As early as January, Major Winchell was making arrangements with a contractor for "a first-class water plant and irrigation system" which was said to cost $9,000 and pump 9000 gallons a minute; both were inflated figures apparently. In April, with population increasing, the Army was still "rushing day and night" to get the irrigation plant into operation. There were setbacks when the artesian well proved too shallow and when the discharge pipe from the pump collapsed due to a cave-in. By June, two pumps were at work. A hundred and fifty acres had been planted in beans, potatoes, and sugar beets, which was less than half what had been anticipated, and the faulty irrigation system could produce only about one-third the amount of water needed. Romie supervised the dropping of more artesian wells, capable of watering three or four acres a day, but crops were late and this was a drought year. The mean annual rainfall of Soledad over twenty-seven years was 8.82 inches; the last few years of the 1890s had been dry and in unirrigated parts of the valley it was reported in 1901 that "practically no crops last seven years."[19] But in 1898, Klondike fever and the Spanish American War boosted prices, so that even partial production looked promising.

In mid-summer, Fort Romie had been visited by Col. Thomas Holland, "the National Colony Overseer," who had orders to superintend a new "Rocky Mountain Chief Division," made up of Colorado, Utah, and New Mexico,[20] of which only Colorado would materialize as a Colony site. In actual practice, Holland would be in charge of the three American farm colonies as they unfolded, and he would act as coordinator, trouble-shooter, and liaison man between colony managers and Booth-Tucker on policy matters. At Romie, Holland was optimistic. He found "everything satisfactory and in flourishing condition, in spite of the drought." Despite such confidence, however, it was clear that the colony was not doing well at the end of its first year and that its financial state was far from healthy. If some of the settlers did clear $200 to $350 above costs, it was primarily from employment outside the colony. If Winchell estimated a total probable income of $5,000 from crops, Booth-Tucker was "not so sanguine" and thought $3,500 would be more realistic.[21]

Besides the drought, there were some internal problems. L. R. Ellert, President of the Sanitary Reduction Works in San Francisco, asked to be relieved of his duties as head of the fund-raising committee, noting that that group had "come to the end of their financial rope." Earlier, Ellert and Wallace Winchell had been embroiled in "a row," as John Milsaps called it, and possibly were still at odds when Ellert stepped down in August of 1898, though he was asked to remain as a member of the committee. In a personal shake-up which was never fully explained, Major Winchell was relieved of his duties as colony superintendent and reassigned; his brother, who also held a post at Fort Romie, was replaced. When the question of Major Winchell came before the Salvation Army's Colonization Board in New York, it reported that "these matters were more or less of a private character" and the matter was referred to Commander Booth-Tucker, "who preferred to deal with it himself." Subsequently, Winchell would become nationally known as an original and innovative officer, famous as the "Bishop of the Bowery" for his work in New York and as an organizer of wartime relief in Belgium in 1915 to 1916.[22]

At the time of Ellert's resignation and Winchell's reassignment, the Army took measures to tighten control of the Soledad colony and to cut costs. When the colonization board, whose functions were largely financial, replaced Winchell with Adjutant and Mrs. Clark, they eliminated one position by transferring stenographic and bookkeeping functions to the Army's divisional accountant. The removal of Winchell's brother saved $13 a week; and in place of a hired engineer, the pumping plant would be overseen by one of the colonists at $1 day when the pump was operating, thus affecting further economy.[23]

The colonists agreed that after paying the balance due the Army for maintenance, they would turn over three-quarters of the year's crops to the colony funds, with the understanding that the colony guarantee maintenance up to the amount handed over at a rate of not more than $3 a week, either in cash or in goods at the option of the colony manager. Money from the sale of settlers' crops was to pay the balance on the pumping system. Booth-Tucker committed national headquarters to a weekly remittance of $50 for colony expenses; requirements above that figure were to be met locally. Within a year or two, the Army contributions dropped to $40 a week, a stipend which continued at least to 1910 and which was important to the settlement's well-being.

Colonists might also rent an additional ten acres, to a total of twenty, paying the usual rate for water and giving the normal crop share as rent. Part of the remaining land was in the home farm, operated by Army personnel; the balance was to be leased to tenants who might occupy empty cottages and up to twenty acres, but would not be eligible for maintenance support. The original settlers were ultimately to receive title to their land for $60 an acre; future settlers would have to pay at least $75, a recognition of increasing land values. Until land and cottage were paid for, the colonist was required to plant at least two-thirds of his fields in crops approved by the manager, with a special recommendation for the growing of sugar beets for the Spreckels plant. Horses and cows owned by the Army were to be turned over to settlers "at reasonable rates," except for a few needed at the home farm and orchard. The Army also maintained a store to supply colonists with strictly staple goods.[24]

Arrangements had to be made to meet payments falling due in October 1898. The Army was currently leasing the property and had not yet purchased it outright. Charles Romie agreed to accept the rental money, half in cash and half in notes. Romie had also financed the irrigation plant and payment of the $2,925 the Army owed because that had already been deferred once. When Romie insisted that this bill be met, the Army colonization board authorized funds for that purpose but instructed Major Winchell (who remained until after harvest) that he should present the money to Romie and at the same time solicit from him "the best donation that he can possibly give towards our Harvest Festival."[25]

Given the lateness of planting and the shortage of water, harvest of potatoes, beans, and hay was considered respectable, though only colonists employed on the side prospered even in a limited way. While most were no doubt grateful for the opportunity of a fresh start, as Winchell was quick to point out, there had been "some trouble" with at least three ingrates who refused to work.[26]

Despite continuing drought and insufficient irrigation water, reporters and visiting Salvation Army officers especially hailed Fort Romie as an example of what imagination and industry might accomplish. When Emma Booth-Tucker included the colony in her extensive western tour early in 1899, both the San Francisco press and the

New York edition of *The War Cry* featured the Consul's visit in positive stories carried under glowing headlines:"Success of the Salvation Army Colony."[27] Booth-Tucker himself swept the West Coast in the summer of 1900, convening "a rousing Holiness Rally" in San Francisco, a "Grand Assault on the Citadels of Sin" at Oakland and an "all day camp on the Farm Colony at Fort Romie," where he visited each cottage personally and held religious meetings twice. Two months later, the Commander lauded the colony in London and distributed press photographs of its buildings.[28]

By that time, most of the nearly 520 acres were under cultivation. The pumping plant, a sixteen-inch, centrifugal pump powered by an eighty-horsepower Frick wood-burning steam engine, was capable of moving on an ordinary run 5,000 gallons a minute through a high trestle flume from the Salinas River, enough to irrigate eight acres in twelve hours but still not adequate. Actually the pump could have doubled its capacity, but the flume could not carry any more. An Indian engineer, perhaps a friend of Booth-Tucker, stopped by to give professional irrigation advice. The Army home farm continued, operated by Staff Captain W. P. Wood, aided by Captains Irwin Alger and Herbert Carleton, plus "Brother" Post, of San Francisco. When the U.S. census-taker made the rounds in 1900, he found a dozen colonists still hard at work, independent and optimistic but admittedly "not making money fast."[29]

Continuing drought cut crop production, and one by one the original colonists drifted away, so that in 1901, three years after the beginning, only one of the "first" families remained. The initial phase of the Fort Romie experiment was over and it could not be called a success in an economic sense. Indeed, as novelist H. Rider Haggard wrote in 1905, after he was asked to evaluate the American colonies: "The result was an utter failure," which cost the Army some $27,000.[30]

In explaining what happened, Salvation Army spokesmen saw several contributing factors. Some of the original colonists, Booth-Tucker noted later, had not been suitable and had turned out to be poor farmers. But generally it was not so much the incompatability of these city "out-of-works" to rural life that brought misfortune; it was primarily circumstance. From the beginning a lack of capital had hampered the experiment and forced the Army to concentrate its monies on the larger tract in Colorado. The $25,000 for starting the colony had not materialized; a loan of $10,000 on which the enterprise had begun had been recalled unexpectedly, so that the Army had been hard pressed to make payments on the land. The Spanish American War had diverted public interest as well as funds, although the *War Cry* editor denied that the conflict had "taken the wind out of the Salvation

Army colony enterprises." The war, plus the drought, had "retarded, but did not kill" the effort.[31] Three years of unmitigated drought, with inadequate water facilities were conditions under which settlers "must have starved had they been the most skilled agriculturists in the world," according to the sympathetic Haggard. This experience, said Haggard, proved nothing about resettling the urban poor on the land: "It leaves the whole question very much where it was." Because of the successive dry seasons, Colonization Director Thomas Holland explained, the early colonists "really did not have fighting chance." And when they returned to the city, leaving the Army in the red, they left behind a net interest in land, livestock, equipment, and improvements that averaged about $1,000 each more than their liabilities.[32]

In the face of this initial setback, the Army regrouped. By a general bond issue, it established its colonies on a more substantial financial base. For Fort Romie, it acquired additional irrigation water from the Monterey Water Company, and it would expand its own pumping system into a colonist-owned and controlled operation, its water of necessity tied to each individual piece of land. It would bring in a second wave of colonization, this time of families with farm backgrounds to be settled on twenty acres each at $100 per acre, payable over a twenty-year period at interest of five percent. Livestock and implements went to the new settlers on a five-year pay schedule, at six percent interest.[33]

At least ten of the newcomers were at Romie by the time the Census of 1900 was taken. Only two recognizable old settlers remained, and one of them, Swedish-born Nils Hamrens would soon leave. Of the dozen families of 1900, their heads averaged 40.8 years of age and all were married except Ede Harding, who at 41 was a widower with four children. Although at least two of the families were childless, the average number of children per family was 2.92. Heads of families were evenly divided between those born abroad and those born in the United States. Of the native-born, Virginia and Missouri each produced two, Louisiana and Iowa one each. Among the foreign born, Scandinavians prevailed: three came from Sweden, one each from Denmark, Finland, and Switzerland.[34]

Those on the scene were augmented by new colonists arriving mainly in the spring of 1901. This new mix, with only Frank O. Lindstrand remaining of the class of 1897, was described as poor folk "living in this district." Men of limited capital, if any at all, they were chosen because they were familiar with agriculture and with conditions in the Salinas Valley. Experience, the rising price of California land and the expense of developing an irrigation system had convinced the Army that some knowledge of farming was essential. Perhaps on the cheap Colorado lands at Fort Amity, the neophyte might have a better opportunity. In 1905, there were still twenty families at Fort Romie. Two additional ones had arrived but left without planting a crop; one man left because of ill-health, accentuated by the climate. But all those of the 1900–1901 influx were still on the scene.[35]

This was the group that H. Rider Haggard would call "a great success." Booth-Tucker referred to them as the "Pilgrim Fathers of Fort Romie," a "splendid group of young men" and "true types of American womanhood." In 1903, the Fort Romie families included thirteen of American background, two Scandinavian and one each of Finnish, German, Swiss, Dutch, and Italian. As Booth-Tucker put it,

> There was the American dash and enterprise, the Dutch plod, the Italian quickness and attention to detail, the Swiss cheeriness and frugality, and the Scandinavian undauntedness, all uniting to solve this great problem of the nations.[36]

A few of the new group came with meager capital. Thomas Bryant was an exception: he came with $1,000. Emil Baetschen (generally known as Carl), a Swiss-German with seven children, who had previously been employed by the Salvation Army as a dairyman, came with a capital of $525. Ari James arrived with a total of $175: Winfield J. Scott had $30 and a team of horses. Most were like Samuel Handley, a former railroad worker who had six children but no capital—"unless children could be called capital." Ex-factory laborer Arioslo Carle owed $30; and Robert Mitchell, a Salvation Army officer who worked in the Army printing plant in San Francisco, came on borrowed money and went deeper into debt when a broken leg put him out of action during most of his first year.[37]

How much actual farm experience was represented is hard to say. C. M. Hodges, in his mid-fifties and older than most, had been a schoolteacher but admitted having "done a little farming" earlier. Missourian Ede Harding had previously lived on a "squat" of 160 acres of dry land. New York native Winfield J. Scott had worked as a hired hand and had farmed on a small scale; while Charles Handley had once homesteaded government land. Not all claimed twenty acres on a gradual payment plan. Allen Roddick, a relative latecomer who had previously worked in the woods, agreed to take up twelve acres of dry land at $38 an acre over a dozen years: this was a tract unsuitable for irrigation but useful for raising poultry. Unique, too, was the Dane, Mathias Mathiesen, who with his wife and five children were at Romie. Rather than pay for the normal allotment over twenty years, Mathiesen in 1903 purchased the Army's home farm of thirty acres, with orchard, for a cash price of $4,650, and in 1905 was one of only two colonists not in debt to the Army.[38]

With few exceptions, almost all of the new wave were married. Widower Ede Harding and the young Salvationist officers who worked on the home farm until it was sold were without wives, as was John Vrieling, who moved from the Army's Ohio colony to Fort Amity in Colorado and then to Romie on account of ill-health. On seven acres, Vrieling raised chickens and in early 1903 obliterated his single status by marrying Maggie Grant of the Colorado colony.[39] It was the Army's firm belief that it was a mistake to colonize the unmarried poor. "The single man is too much like a rolling stone," said Booth-Tucker; "very often he is here to-day and gone to-morrow." Moreover, it was comparatively easy to take care of the unmarried poor in the cities. As for colonization, family life was "a sheet-anchor to the scheme," the Commander insisted. "The family will prove cheaper in the long run, since the wife and children supply unpaid labor." If the husband were able to work as a carpenter building barns or cottages in the settlement, his spouse and their offspring could tend to the home and fields while he brought in a cash income.[40] Thus large families were to be encouraged, as in rural America in general. In instances where the husband died before his commitments to the Army were met, the wife might take over, which several of them did with both diligence and success.[41]

Under the astute management of Staff-Captain Nels Erikson beginning in 1902, Fort Romie began to prosper. Erikson reported in mid-September that a new era was at hand: "Colony affairs are progressing nicely and I am glad to state that conditions at Romie are much improved and the Colonists are in good spirits."[42]

Although the drought years were now behind them, the Army further developed the irrigation system. By deed in 1902, it acquired the water rights of the Monterey Water Company at or near Fort Romie. About the same time, it converted its wood-burning pumping engine to fuel oil, signing a contract with Standard Oil in a drive for both efficiency and economy.[43] Since November 1899, when the Army ceased its lease and acquired the Romie property outright, Charles Romie had promised to deed over a 150 by 300 foot plot for the pumping plant, plus a twenty-foot right-of-way to the river. But Romie consistently dragged his heels. ". . . It was one excuse after another," reported the legal counsel in New York, who noted, ". . . I have had more correspondence on that one thing, trying to get old Romie to do it, than I have had with any other matter pertaining to any of the colonies all put together." The Army's attorney in Soledad "had everything else but a regular scrap with him, but all of no use." But in April 1903, Romie made good his promise, actually giving the Army more land than promised, a twenty-five-foot right-of-way and an area

175 by 345 feet for the pump equipment. "Evidently Romie is beginning to realize that he is nearing the end and had better try and make his account for the great Hereafter as easy to meet as possible," wrote the cynical Madison Ferris, the lawyer in New York.[44]

Seeking to withdraw from some of its commitments, Salvation Army officers, especially Thomas Holland, suggested that the irrigation project be taken over entirely by the colonists themselves. In the spring of 1903, after "considerable negotiation" and hesitance on the settlers' part, an agreement was reached and the Romie Water Company was incorporated as a colonist-owned vehicle. Nels Erikson was President; other officers included Ede Harding, Ari James, W. W. Boswell, and Samuel Handley. The Army formally sold the water system to the Romie Water Company (in Army records always the Fort Romie Water Company) for $6,750, this figure based on one $15-share of stock for each irrigable acre. The cost of such shares was added to each settler's indebtedness to the Army, to be carried without interest for twenty years. Thus at $15 a share, a colonist with twenty acres would have to have paid in $300 before land title could pass to him. On its part, the company agreed to furnish water, keep the system repaired and insured for at least $1,000 and the taxes paid upon it. Failure to contribute his regular share could bring the loss of whatever equity a colonist might have in the company by virtue of payments already made. Only landowners could hold stock. Shares were assigned as security for payment of stockholders notes given in exchange to the water company, which in turn assigned the share certificates to the Salvation Army. If a colonist disposed of his property to a third party, the shares transferred; if his right to the land reverted to the Army, so also did the company shares.[45]

Twenty colonists came under this arrangement, along with Mathiesen who fell in a special category because of his outright land purchase. With the principle of ownership and control of the irrigation system attached irrevocably to the soil, the Romie Water Company took over the improved equipment, which by now included more than three-and-a-half miles of main ditches.[46] During the life of the colony, the scheme seemed to work satisfactorily. Only in the 1930s would there be minor litigation because the deeds drawn from the Salvation Army to settlers neglected to reserve the water easement in the water company.[47]

When Commander Booth-Tucker visited Fort Romie in May 1903 and was up all night after being feted at a midnight banquet, he expressed himself as "very pleased" with the progress he saw. The irrigation system was on a sound basis and many colonists used windmills to augment their water supply. Another Farmers' Institute had been held a few months earlier by University of California specialists, although an outbreak of measles had caused cancellation of the usual Christmas gathering and Santa Claus had arrived on a hayrack instead of a sleigh. Booth-Tucker reported that $6,000 worth of milk per year was being sold to the local cheese factory and that one settler was contemplating a cheese plant of his own. One colonist had realized $1,000 from his twenty acres, "besides getting a good living for himself and family," and excellent returns were being made from livestock and poultry—the average per family estimated at around $850 per year.[48]

By October 1904, there were twenty-four families at Romie, including tradespeople. Townsite buildings included the Salvation Army Hall, D. W. Wiley's cheese factory, Joseph Gilkey's blacksmith shop, and a cooperative store organized on the Rochdale plan, a not uncommon American phenomenon at the turn of the century.[49] The general merchandise store, the Fort Romie Rochdale Company, had been incorporated in April and was scheduled to open on the morning of May 24, 1904, after "a special literary and musical program" and with speakers explaining the principles on which it was founded. Open to members and nonmembers alike, the store was subsidized by the Army, which provided a rent-free building and invested $200 in company shares. It was managed by a former Oregon legislator, and it boasted "an up-to-date stock of fresh, clean and new merchandise at prices that are right." The manager of the colony, Nels Erikson, was also president of the company, which exchanged goods in kind as well as on a cash basis, but offered no credit. Colonists and Army alike sold beef on the hoof to the store's butcher shop and bought a wide range of goods from foodstuffs to milkpails and oilcloth, with dividends to consumers of from five to ten percent.[50]

The Army also underwrote a loan "for Cows" for Fort Romie settlers at the Salinas City Bank, when in 1902 Booth-Tucker agreed to sign a note, after which individual colonists gave their own notes, mortgaging the livestock they purchased in the process. While they were generally prompt to pay the interest on their loans, they did little about the principal, and the bank extended the due date at least twice, once in 1904 and again in 1906.[51]

Visual evidence of progress was clearly obvious. In addition to having its own post office, by 1904 the colony was part of an RFD route, the first in Monterey County, with a colonist carrying the mail. Fort Romie potatoes had been exhibited at the St. Louis World's Fair; and colony visitors were greeted not only by the Army's high-flying flag of black and red with a yellow sunburst and the words "Blood & Fire" on it, but also by an "Evergreen arch of welcome" at the entrance of a newly laid out town park, for which many of the plantings had come from the San Francisco Board of Park Commissioners.[52]

As the company developed, late in 1903 the Army opened negotiations with Charles Romie for additional land, although attorney Madison Ferris in New York advised manager Erikson to proceed with caution. "Romie is an uncertain element always in a deal," he said, "and needs to be tied up as tight as a man can be tied, so that there will be no evasion and matters will be thoroughly understood, as he can crawl through as small a loophole as any man I ever struck in my life."[53] "After considerable nagging," Romie gave the Army a two year lease on 172.05 acres lying between the colony and the river, with an option to purchase for $13,000.[54] Subsequently, when the option was about to expire, Erikson argued in favor of acquiring the land. Since 1900, Romie had "shown a good profit"; the early misfortunes ought to be written off. After all, he said, "God forgives past failures and we might too." Except for weekly managerial expenses, the colony no longer relied upon national headquarters for funds. Local land prices were rising steadily; property worth $17 an acre four years earlier now brought $120 to $125; the colony land was valued at $145 per acre. At $13,000, Erikson argued, it was a bargain; already it was worth about $18,000. A Salinas bank offered to advance $11,000 on a first mortgage, and Erikson believed that he could raise the remaining $2,000 locally. With such an addition fronting on the Salinas River, another forty families could be settled. But for some reason, despite Erikson's urging, the option to buy was never exercised.[55]

Apparently many of the second wave of colonists came without formal contracts with the Army. Sometime in 1903, Colonization Commissioner Thomas Holland and Nels Erikson set to work to remedy this omission and drew up a document they believed fair to both parties. Settlers at first were opposed to the idea of a contract, but mellowed some, and Erikson believed that compromises could be made.[56] Madison Ferris in New York urged pulling "the strings tight" legally. The moment the Army "let the colonist begin to dictate, and tell us what they will have and what they won't have in their contracts," it lost its power and its influence. If the colonists thought the "morality clause" on drunk and disorderly activity too strict, to Ferris that was "the best argument in the world why the clause should not be changed."[57] Once Ferris had cleared the document and the Army's lawyers in Salinas had made a few changes to conform to California law, Erikson brought it before a business meeting of Fort Romie colonists, who passed a resolution approving it. The "morality clause" stayed in, though settlers were assured that it would be liberally defined and that no man would lose his property rights for a single infraction.

The term "to sell" was substituted for "to lease," since no lease in California could be negotiated for more than ten years. The word "lease" had been in the agreements with the original settlers because the Army at that time did not possess title to the land and did not wish to promise more than it could deliver. And, above all, Holland argued, ". . . we don't want these people to imagine themselves tenants." The contract retained the original stipulation, that had never been acted upon, that the Army at its discretion could reserve one-half of a colonist's crop to pay arrears in debt. But it also eliminated a new proposal, suggested by Holland, that the Army receive fifteen percent of the colonist's income from milk, cream, poultry, and hogs. Duly signed by officials in New York, seventeen duplicates of these contracts returned to Fort Romie later in 1904.[58]

Although one modern writer confused him with a "poet feller" named Rudyard Kipling, the Englishman H. Rider Haggard arrived to inspect the colony in March 1905.[59] His visit provided an opportunity to evaluate the experiment, although it must be said that Haggard was a partisan, a staunch back-to-the-land advocate, and his trip was to collect evidence to help convince the British government to subsidize a large-scale Salvation Army colonization program in northwest Canada.[60] The novelist spent two days on the scene poring over individual balance sheets and sworn statements of appraisers and interviewing colonists and Army leaders before arriving at a decidedly optimistic view of the financial status of the colony and its residents.

Of sixteen settlers consulted, six were primarily engaged in raising cattle; two specialized in poultry; five grew potatoes on a commercial basis; several also planted alfalfa regularly; but none mentioned sugar beets. At this time, the Salvation Army still held 130 acres of undistributed land. Using figures that included the rising value of California farmland, Haggard calculated the total value of Fort Romie as $113,280, although the Army's own balance sheets six months later were decidedly more modest and indicated some $80,173.98 in assets of all kinds.[61]

Before he turned over the job to Jacob Romig early in 1906, Staff Captain Nels Erikson had managed the colony for four years. He had provided strong leadership and when reassigned could take pride in having seen the settlement develop "from a poor, struggling dependency into a prosperous community."[62] Fort Romie colonists had a better record than their counterparts in Colorado in meeting their commitments. In 1905, Erikson sketched out the hypothetical debt of the individual settler: $2,250 for land and buildings, $270 for accrued interest, $300 for horses and cattle, and $100 for the general fund to repay living advances. Part of the debt was designed to be liquidated in the first three years, but the bulk ran for twenty. With an easy payment plan at first, the rate of payments might go to $20 a month for the rest of the period; if a colonist assumed a second ten acres, with everything included—land, buildings, livestock, irrigation, and general fund—$40 a month or nearly $500 a year would not be uncommon.[63]

With one inexplicable exception, 1913, the Fort Romie Loan Account, that is, the debts owed by the California colony to the national headquarters of the Salvation Army, showed a steady shrinkage.[64]

1907	$31,980.61	1912	$15,311.10
1909	30,718.78	1913	18,702.49
1910	23,585.04	1916	11,754.92
1911	$17,108.23		

Perhaps not as prosperous as Haggard would have his readers believe, the colony was, nonetheless, over its difficult days. Settlers were moving slowly toward gaining title to their own land, although most did not achieve that goal until the 1910–1917 era.

CHAPTER FIVE

Fort Amity, Colorado

Back to the land, back to the land,
We're happy colonists, now on the land,
Won't you come and join us, leave the city's din,
There is joy and Amity back on the land.[1]

WHILE FORT ROMIE WAS DEVELOPING at a modest pace, the Salvation Army was pouring more of its resources into its second colony, Fort Amity, located in the Arkansas Valley in southeastern Colorado. A few miles west of the town of Holly, the property was on the mountain branch of the Santa Fe Trail. An old trading post and stage station was located there and the main line of the Santa Fe railroad was half a mile away. The land itself had been part of Hiram Holly's SS ranch. It had subsequently been owned by a British cattle syndicate which had failed, after which a few dry-land farmers had tried their luck on parts of it before giving up in 1887.[2]

Meanwhile, important eastern businessmen, including Henry B. Hyde of the Equitable Life Insurance Company, General Louis Fitzgerald of the Mercantile Trust Company, and New York gun manufacturer Marcellus Hartley, organized the Great Plains Water Company to develop the lower Arkansas Valley for irrigated settlement. Eventually, under the personal supervision of former New York insurance broker William M. Wiley, the concern constructed 150 miles of canals, 750 miles of laterals and a 14,000-acre storage reservoir, all at a cost of nearly $3,000,000. By the end of the century, when it was advertising widely for settlers, it was considered "the largest irrigation enterprise in the United States."[3]

It was from the Amity Land Company, an affiliate of the Great Plains Water Company, that the Army acquired its original 640-acre colony site in Colorado which was all of Section 12, Township 23 South, of Range 43 West. The land carried perpetual water rights derived from the Buffalo Creek Canal to the north at an annual fee and an assessment for maintenance. With William Wiley and William N. Coler, Jr., both active on its behalf, the firm was promoting "Irrigated Farms For Sale" in newspapers as far away as Chicago. Apparently the Salvation Army made no down payment and quoted the price at $20 per acre, plus water at fifty cents an acre per year. Although concluded in September of 1897, this contract seemingly was not recorded at the time, but documents filed in 1901, after the land had been refinanced, indicated that the total cost had been $13,307.50 or $20.79 per acre.[4]

Once the land had been secured, the Army rapidly mobilized its forces to select and settle colonists. In both tasks, the key figure seems to have been Thomas Holland. Regarded as the "father" of Fort Amity, he was soon to become the national colonization secretary. While the mechanism of choosing settlers is not clear, Holland certainly had a hand as Booth-Tucker possibly did. Later, when colonists were in place in Colorado and California and settlement was about to begin in Ohio, the Commander wrote: "I have been over the list of Colonists and have picked out some very good ones, all market gardeners and a good proportion of Salvationists." But probably Holland played the major role in winnowing the names of the "worthy poor" from reams of unsolicited applications, of which by early 1899 the Army had received more than 5,000, among them hundreds who qualified and were ready to migrate west. As in California, potential settlers received application forms; they were required to give references; and they were interviewed in their homes. In keeping with the nineteenth-century Gospel-of-Wealth tradition, both honesty and industry as well as ability and sobriety were vital personal traits sought in the selection process. Holland, it was said, was a shrewd judge. As a result, "the pioneer group was carefully selected with a view to intelligence, character and physical capacity."[5]

A subsequent observer, however, referred to them as "a motley crowd, all hard up, mustered from all sorts of occupations," most ignorant of farming, with some who "hardly knew one end of a plow from the other." Holland insisted otherwise. All of the original colonists except five had at some time worked on farms, even though for the moment they were city dwellers. All were married and most had children; and they represented a wide spectrum of occupations—from laborer, warehouseman, and wagon driver to painter, plasterer, carpenter, tailor, and streetcar conductor. Added later were a few "pacesetters" and "examples," who were more experienced farmers from Colorado, Kansas, or Missouri. In general, they were not of the hardcore pauper class; the Army deemed them deserving poor with small opportunity in the city. Eleven of the first fourteen families actually came from Chicago and one each from Kansas City, Cleveland, and Alliance, Ohio.[6]

Once the colonists were chosen, Holland and other Army Officers organized the logistics and procured goods in Chicago. By boxcar, they shipped 2,200 pounds of groceries bought from Sprague Warner at a cost of $88.74; hardware from Hibbard and Spencer (cost—$216.80); $1,153.95 worth of lumber from the Harris Lumber Company; and implements, harness, and tools costing $799 from Studebaker, Leonard, and Bradley. To purchase and ship twenty-three horses to Holly cost $509.[7]

Holland moved quickly. "You might have called us the 'Salvation Army Flying Squadron,'" he noted, "for if we did not actually fly, we got there as quickly as it is possible to travel without wings."[8] On April 16, 1898, Holland and a fellow officer—probably Ensign Nels Erikson—arrived in Colorado to supervise the details of land plotting and distribution. Two days later the main body of colonists steamed into Holly aboard a Santa Fe train at 2 A.M. while rain poured down "by the bucketful." Newspaper accounts disagree as to their numbers, but Army records indicate that there were fourteen families, plus Army personnel.[9] Colonel Holland's cash book specifies that the Salvation Army paid the rail fare of twenty-four colonist family members; many small children rode free. When Staff Captain James Burrows, whose family may already have come, arrived eleven days after the first wave, he found fifty-two people at the new Fort Amity, as it was to be known. The Army also defrayed freight charges for personal and household goods. They ranged from the sixteen dollars it cost to ship Walter Baldwin's 4,000 pounds to the sixty cents for Chris Christenson's 150-pound chest. But Christenson came alone, Baldwin with a wife and seven children. A new Baldwin daughter, Eva Amity, was the first child born at the colony.[10]

Household goods, implements, and other freight were delayed, even though shipped in advance, and colonists had to wait three days in Holly; the women and children slept in a first-class passenger car, by courtesy of the Santa Fe Railroad, while the men slept on hay in a boxcar. During the waiting, Holland recorded an outlay of $15.55 for sundries such as buckets, basins, towels, bedticking, milk, bread, and eggs, which like the freight and travel charges were to be prorated among the colonists and eventually repaid to the Army.[11] When their freight arrived, according to Holland, "our little company of pioneers" rode in the still-continuing rain to the colony land, "an untouched prairie wilderness." One wife remembered it as "just a Barren open space," a vista the Denver press thought gave the country "a wild, desolate appearance."[12]

Living conditions were primitive. Until houses were built, the settlers lived in tents brought from Chicago or in the abandoned stage-station trading post on the site. Holland bunked in a tent with a Chicago family, with curtains hung for mutual privacy, then moved to a makeshift office-store-bedroom which he shared with other Salvation Army personnel. This "headquarters shanty," he described as

> . . . just a trifle bigger than the dining-room in our home in Jersey City. In one corner sleep Staff Capt. Burrows and his boy, high up on a shelf over a potato bin. On another still higher shelf sleep Erikson and myself; further on, the two Capts. Davey [sic] and about half-a-dozen others.
>
> Over our heads hang an interesting mixture of stove-pipe fittings, harness and sundry hardware supplies, while another part makes an excellent show as a general country store.
>
> The evenings are made merry with plenty of song, prayer and testimony, with a plentiful mixture of cornet, harp and guitar. Altogether, we are a happy family.[13]

From his "headquarters shanty," Holland supervised the establishment of Fort Amity. "His skin tanned as brown as a coffee berry, fire flashing from his coal-black eyes and nerves at high tension," he was a man of optimism, practicality, and versatility who proved to be an inspiring leader. For a time, as "full-blown Governor" at the settlement, Holland directed colonists and fellow officers alike. Ensign Nels Erikson served as "a splendid A.D.C.," acting as secretary, storekeeper, and "general factotum," according to the full-bearded Staff Captain James Burrows, who was a colonist as well as an official. The two Davy brothers, both captains, were also part of the original cadre. One, A.J., known as John, met Holland in Kansas City and joined the original settlers to oversee the installation of the irrigation system; Wallace was in charge of agriculture in general. On his own, Holland was said to have "acquired a thorough knowledge" of conditions in Colorado and was "therefore prepared to manage the work along scientific lines."[14]

Two of the men cooked breakfast, and the women prepared the other meals, a diet generally heavy on eggs, bacon, and pancakes. Holland split his work force. One group, headed by the stone mason

and four carpenters among the colonists, concentrated on the construction of homes; the others worked to break sod and plant crops. In
addition, a Salvationist from Denver, a market gardener, gave general
agricultural advice, and another layman helped build a number of the
first houses before becoming a Salvation Army cadet in the Colorado
capital. It was typical of Holland's organizational abilities that David
Coker, a Chicago painter who had once been a bandsman, blew the
bugle calls at 6 A.M. for breakfast and half an hour later for work, which
continued with a noon break until 6 P.M.[15]

With the twenty-three horses accompanying the first group, settlers worked to prepare the soil and were joined by local farmers hired
to help break the tough prairie sod. Holland later admitted that it had
been a mistake not to have had the land broken before the colonists
arrived. The first year was planned with an emphasis on the production
of garden crops, especially onions and cantaloupes, the seeds of which
Holland had obtained in Pueblo. Along with readying the soil and
planting, the group also had to be concerned with construction of
laterals, ditches, and headgates to distribute irrigation water from the
Buffalo Canal.[16]

Holland himself marveled as the newcomers "caught up chaos and
molded it to form and life." Outside observers were amazed at the
industry of the colonists and the lack of complaint, despite bad weather
and a sea of mud. They were astonished, too, to find a construction
crew "which did not engage in cursing and swearing."[17] In late May,
they noted that seven breakers and three pulverizers were running
from dawn to dark and that more than eighty acres had been planted in
melons and several more in truck garden. Ten houses were up and
others on the way. Truly, said the editor of the *Holly Chieftain*, "The
Salvation Army colonists are making things hum." By mid-August,
when Commander Booth-Tucker made his first visit, nearly a square
mile had been transformed. The Commander was delighted. In a
"lengthy address," he told the colonists that their initial successes had
dispelled the "doubt and distrust" of many Americans and had paved
the way for additional settlers.[18]

Despite Holland's first joint effort, prompted by the late spring
start, the heart of the plan was small-scale individual land allotment.
"There is no community scheme about it," explained Salvation Army
secretary, Lieutenant Colonel Richard Holz. "Each person is to be
treated as an individual, and must work out his own destiny with the
same advantages as his neighbor or give up." The plan was cooperative,
he said, but "it stops at the door of each man's home."[19] Thus, like the
colonists at Fort Romie, each man signed a contract with the Army,
agreeing to farm ten acres at a yearly rental of $2 per acre, with title to

be transferred at the end of eleven years when payment had totaled $22.50 an acre, plus six percent interest. The land was divided into sixty-four ten-acre lots, each 320 feet wide and a quarter of a mile long, so that a section made four rows of lots, sixteen in each row. When houses were placed in a line, twenty rods on either side of the road, the appearance of a compact street was obtained. At the same time, the Army reserved each alternate lot to rent or to sell to a colonist on adjoining property.[20]

Each man was provided with a house, according to the size of his family. A couple with one child might receive a fourteen-by-eighteen foot two-room cottage; a family of five might occupy a three-room house. The largest houses planned for families with as many as nine children had nine rooms.[21] Initially each colonist was furnished with a horse and a cow, along with a variety of equipment, including harness, shovel plow, nine-inch stirring plow, hand implements, five-shovel cultivator, spring-tooth harrow, one-horse Studebaker wagon and seed drill, "all bran new."[22] During the first year, while work focused mainly on breaking land, building houses, and running irrigation ditches, the Army also subsidized familes with cash loans averaging from two dollars to four dollars a week. All Army advances for transportation, land, housing, equipment, livestock, and living expenses were to be repaid, and toward this end, Holland kept a running account for each colonist. This was not charity, Secretary Holz pointed out. "People who cannot support themselves must go to some one of our other institutions. The colony is a place for workers."[23]

As soon as possible, most settlers expanded their lease holdings to twenty acres, with ultimate option to purchase, inasmuch as the Army did not yet hold full title to the property. Each contract contained the same "half-crop clause" included at Fort Romie (but never used at either colony) that allowed the Army to retain up to half of the proceeds of each group to pay for rent arrears. Each settler agreed to plant and to irrigate shade trees and to accept the "morality clause" prohibiting alcohol and endorsing "sobriety, industry and faithfulness to the interest and welfare of the Colony."[24]

Although crops were late in 1898, by hard work and cooperation the colonists planted eighty acres of cantaloupes, a product Holland considered a market staple, but whose price fluctuated greatly based on supply and demand. Nat Wetzel, a St. Louis commission agent, had contracted with the growers' association at Holly to ship thirty-seven cars of cantaloupes, 400 crates per car, for a price of ninety-nine and a half cents a crate. While the Amity colonists were not formal parties to this agreement, undoubtedly they knew they could market all they produced. The melon crop was excellent, and in August Booth-Tucker reported "a very favorable prospect in crops," conservatively estimating a return of $3,500 for the season. So encouraged was he, that he was seeking to acquire additional adjoining land and was enthusiastically proposing expansion of the irrigation system and the introduction of a poultry specialist with the idea of raising chickens for the market.[25]

Then adversity struck. As the cantaloupes matured, a glut reduced prices sharply; Wetzel's firm failed, and the colonists lost at least $1,500 on melons handled by this agency. In addition, on September 5, a frost killed the rest of the crop before it was harvested, and the remainder of the yield was destroyed. Thus the first year's cantaloupe crop was an almost total loss; only enough vegetables were produced to last through the winter.[26]

Given this first setback, colonists were supported by continuing Salvation Army loans, by the products of their root cellars, by income from other jobs, and by tightening their belts. A number of men earned money working on a reservoir some forty miles away; a stone mason made $3.50 a day at his trade; a shoemaker, who had learned his skills in Chicago, brought in $1.00 a day mending shoes and "making leggings for the cowboys." Mrs. Erik Erickson advertised her talents as a dressmaker, with "Latest Styles" and "Superior Worksmanship"; David Coker reverted to his calling as a wallpaper hanger and house- and sign-painter, while others hung out their shingles as plasterers or carpenters.[27]

By Christmas 1898, Fort Amity had a school house, a post office, a general store, a tailor shop, and a hall for lectures, entertainment or religious services. Despite the cantaloupe disaster, Commander Booth-Tucker was convinced that a breakthrough had been made. Subtitles to his interview with a *New York Herald* reporter in December made that clear: "Booth-Tucker Believes That He has Solved the Problem That Has Baffled the Ages"; "The Success of the Colony Exceeds my Best Expectations." He described some of the changes among the Amity colonists, especially the women and children.

> The weary haunted look seen in their eyes when they came, the drawn, hard lines of their faces, have all disappeared, and instead you see pink cheeks, quiet smiling eyes, which bespeak well nourished bodies, steady nerves and a hopeful condition of mind.

With success already demonstrated and with an additional $50,000 in capital, Booth-Tucker believed he could "prove to a mathematical certainty that the scheme is socially and morally, as well as financially, safe." The settlers were "earnest, honest workers and I want to put one hundred and fifty thousand such men in the Colorado Valley," he said.[28]

When Colonel Holland was interviewed in Kansas City early in 1899, he announced that new families were being added at Fort Amity, "in one of the best irrigation districts in the world." Bubbling with optimism, he did not ignore the first year cantaloupe loss, but because of diversified farming, he promised, it would not happen again. The single family cow would give way to several, and a creamery was planned for the following season. Sheeps and hogs would be introduced. More alfalfa would be grown and onions planted for the first time. And two experienced gardeners were coming from Kalamazoo, Michigan, to introduce celery, which seemed to thrive in alkaline soil.[29]

The Salvation Army's "Fall and Winter Campaign" of 1898 lauded its farm colonies in general and postulated 100 additional families of settlers "to become home owners" on an easy installment plan. So bright was the outlook, that the editor of the western *War Cry* predicted that "the entire pauper system of the United States will soon be run on this principle, and that of the civilized world."[30]

Immediate expansion at Fort Amity was on a more modest scale. As early as the fall of 1898, Booth-Tucker was negotiating with the Amity Land Company for the half-section immediately to the south of its original 640 acres to bring the colony "right across the railroad," which had agreed to put in a switch and a depot to save carting products six miles to Holly.[31] By a contract of 1899, part of this half-section—307.8 acres—was acquired, as was 46.65 acres which passed from the Amity Land Company to Lou B. Rand in 1901 and subsequently to the Army. And also in 1901 the company sold the Army an additional 835.54 acres, making a total of 1,829.99 acres in the Fort Amity settlement.[32]

As land holdings grew, so did the number of colonists. Figures are not firm: settlers moved in and out, and even Salvation Army leaders could not always agree on the count. Early in 1899, Booth-Tucker reported that there were thirty-seven families living in good houses at Amity, but probably his figure was too high. In June of the same year Thomas Holland counted twenty-six families—150 souls and "a hardworking, earnest, painstaking lot." The census of 1900 was to show twenty-nine families, including the Army manager and five renters. Booth-Tucker, visiting about the same time, predicted a doubling in size during the coming year, with thirty new stone cottages contemplated by the spring of 1901.[33] These numbers never did materialize; nor did the Commander's later forecasts of 300 or even 450 men, women, and children. When a distinguished British visitor surveyed the colony in 1905 he found thirty-eight families, including six renters or tenants.[34]

But despite a certain amount of turnover and a consistent population of around thirty bona fide colonist families, Fort Amity grew

physically and seemed to prosper. Its agricultural emphasis was on
diversity and a broader economic base. It was announced at the beginning of 1899, for example, that each family would be provided with
"five well bred dairy cows," with a creamery to be established in the
spring, and that many fruit and shade trees were soon to be planted.
Colonel Holland said the same thing in different words when he
reported that he had just paid out $5,000 "for a splendid lot of dairy
cows, and what with the delicious fodder from our fields, we shall soon
be presenting our cheeses and other dairy products to the market."[35]
Later that same year, the Army's Finance Council in New York approved funds of $200 for lumber to build cattle sheds and a creamery
building; it also provided $145 for creamery machinery and $250 to
meet a note coming due on the plant. Illustrations circulating in England late in 1900 showed a number of wooden buildings at the colony,
including a combined creamery-blacksmith shop—probably a skim-
ming station rather than a full-fledged creamery. But with the Army
pushing the idea, providing dairy cows and eventually a Holstein bull
and a stone building near the rail line, by 1903, colonists were delivering some 1,000 pounds a day and were shipping either through the
Amity Creamery Company or the Continental Creamery of Topeka.[36]
Records indicate that the Army consistently subsidized livestock and
especially dairy animals. "A cow for colonist Langdon"—$30—is a
typical entry. It purchased a veterinary supply outfit and "a Vaccine
instrument" which was put to good use in the springs of 1900 and 1902
when Blackleg struck the herds. Three years later, when the same
disease caused losses, the Army gave grants of $50 and $100 each to
several owners, to be used against their livestock loan accounts.[37] By
1905, a few settlers had dairy herds of from fifteen to twenty head,
although a modern newspaper source argues that dairying and the
local cheese factory were never profitable because of the poor grade of
cattle at the colony.[38]

Hogs also early became a family staple but commercial sheep
raising arrived relatively late in 1905, when Louis H. Kephart of New
Mexico purchased forty acres at Amity because he "liked the community, the absence of liquor and good moral surroundings in general and
because the area seemed to offer an excellent oportunity to grow
sheep." Because of his experience, Kephart became a kind of "pace
setter," demonstrating in practice that profits were to be made by
shipping sheep to Kansas City.[39]

As early as the autumn of 1898, Booth-Tucker had noted that it was
impossible to buy chickens in Holly and that "millions of dollars" worth
of poultry were brought into Colorado from Kansas each year, a fact
which posed excellent trade prospects for the colony. At one point, the
Commander had hoped to develop an extensive poultry-farming pro-

gram, not only for the colonies but for the Army's Children's Homes and Rescue Homes as well. In fact, he confided to his brother-in-law in 1899, "I am sending two or three Salvationists to take a course in Poultriology in a Poultry College near New York."[40] Most colonists raised chickens for their own use or for egg-money. Staff Captain Joseph H. Hargreaves was the Amity specialist, though no graduate of a Poultry College. A veteran of twenty-one years in the Salvation Army, Hargreaves came to the colony with health problems "as a last resort." His ailing lungs improved, and with the usual subsidy, he farmed and raised chickens. Early in 1902, his incubators were full for hatching and he had orders for "hundreds of thoroughbred hen's eggs" from other settlers. Three years later, he had 150 chickens and was running forty acres in alfalfa, beets, and cantaloupes, a crop combination which came to dominate colony agriculture.[41]

In 1905 when Haggard made his survey, the twenty farmers listed their products in descending order of importance: sugar beets, alfalfa, grain, cantaloupes, livestock, poultry, fruit, and beets. All families grew their own gardens and the Army, with some consistency, laid out funds for seed. One colony manager tinkered with a greenhouse and encouraged the planting of sorghum and Kaffir corn; when the Army gave its annual prizes in September of 1900, there were winners in those categories as well as general gardening, onions, cauliflower, horses, cows and calves, poultry and hogs. In 1902, one colonist raised sixty-five acres of broomcorn, perhaps some of it at least for Frank McAbee's new broom factory, the first products of which "went like hot cakes" at J. H. Childs' Amity store.[42]

The various dairy herds or Charles Barkman's thirty-two beef animals or J. A. Ziegler's forty-five head, plus every family's supply of livestock, made hay and feed grains important crops. Settlers planted fifty acres of sorghum for winter feed in 1901, but alfalfa, wheat, and oats were most popular. In a good season, irrigated land produced four cuttings of alfalfa hay and the colony had a surplus for sale. The Army's home farm and its nonassigned land rented to settlers on a share basis meant that Holland could advertise alfalfa in local newspapers. Wheat and rye and occasionally a car of "fine oats" were shipped to market by rail.[43]

In 1900, despite the 1898 disaster, cantaloupes were one of the two main crops. Sugar beets was the other. At first, colonists shipped through the Holly Cantaloupe Growers Association, to which many belonged. The establishment of a melon-loading shed at Amity was a great boon to local growers, who soon restructured into such groups as the Amity Cantaloupe Growers Association, the Amity Dairy and Produce Association, and the Sugar Beet Growers Association in efforts to bargain more effectively with railroad and consignment firms. With more than 300 acres in cantaloupes in the spring of 1901, the Amity growers were concerned about net returns on each car shipped, rather than a pro rata price for the entire season; they were bothered by sharp increases in shipping rates without warning; and they used their Association as a forum to air numerous other grievances and to determine which commission agents to use. Colonists sat on the board of directors and Colonel Holland was elected a market committeeman.[44]

The crop varied. In 1902, a good year, the first cantaloupes were consigned east in mid-August, with three additional cars sent out in early September. At the same time, the association also shipped a carload of watermelons, a more risky commodity because of price fluctuations. But the 1903 crop fell victim to natural disaster. According to Holland, it "was almost completely killed off by hail."[45] This was one more reason why growers were gradually switching to other crops and by 1905 only four of the twenty colonists who responded specifically to Haggard's query were planting cantaloupes.

By now the most important cash crop was sugar beets. The beet sugar industy of Colorado had boomed at a remarkable rate in the early twentieth century. In 1900 investors underwrote two separate factories, one at Sugar City, north of Rocky Ford, and one at Rocky Ford itself. In 1901, the Oxnard brothers, with substantial sugar interests in California and Nebraska, joined with eastern capitalists, including Henry B. Hyde, who was already involved in the Arkansas Valley, to create the Arkansas Valley Sugar Beet and Irrigated Land Company (A.V.S.B. & I.L.C.) to develop land and irrigation facilities and promote sugar beet culture in the eastern end of Colorado. The history of this "alphabetical organization," as it was sometimes called, was intertwined with that of the Amity Land Company and its parent Great Plains Water Company. It seems likely that the Amity-Great Plains combination, whence the Salvation Army acquired its property and rights, had failed and that the A.V.S.B. & I.L.C. emerged after Hyde and his group took over by foreclosure, pouring more money in to protect their already heavy investments. Their object was to divide 120,000 acres into 40-acre irrigated farms to sell at low prices to settlers agreeing to raise ten acres of beets for a period of years, a project that was completed by 1905 at a cost of nearly $3 million, without many of the anticipated buyers materializing.[46]

In 1901, Booth-Tucker noted that the A.V.S.B. & I.L.C.—the legitimate heir of the firms from which the Army had acquired its land and water and the arm of the powerful American Beet Sugar Company—owned all the land near Amity. "In fact we are its tenants." Thus when the company contemplated a large beet processing plant in the area, the Commander saw the advantage. Such a factory, together with development of a tuberculosis sanitarium for working men, "will take all our products and give us a home market," he said. "Amity colony will not be dependent upon railroads or railroad rates." When the company relocated one of its Nebraska plants at Lamar, a few miles to the west, William M. Wiley, who had spearheaded its operations around Holly, brought together capital, much of it from Denver, to establish a rival Holly Sugar Company, which opened its Holly plant in time for the 1905 season.[47]

In 1901 the Amity colonists had planted three times as many sugar beets as in the previous season and with the nearby markets expanding the popularity of the cash crop would grow. Like melons, beets were labor-intensive, and required much hand work—hoeing, thinning, and harvesting. One colony family was able to make thirty dollars a week during the beet-thinning season of 1901; a year later, with thinning at its peak in May, "crowds of men, women and children" could be seen working in the fields. In time, colonist labor would be replaced by migrant workers—Indians, Mexicans, and ultimately California Japanese—although entrepeneurs like Robert Newman and W. Mitchell bought beet planters and contracted to do custom planting in and around Amity.[48]

The railroad was essential to sugar beet growers. By the fall of 1900, Amity had a loading track, freight platform, melon shed, coal house, and scales. The Santa Fe had promised a depot and a siding but was slow to carry through. Meanwhile, it did establish a beet dump to which farmers might bring their product, "unload in about four minutes and be ready to return home." Colonists had invested in the dump and formed an association to regulate its use, giving preferential rates to shareholders over nonmembers until 1907 when they voted to sell their shares to the American Beet Sugar Company.[49]

Colonists grumbled about the railroad, especially the scarcity of beet cars at harvest time. They complained, too, about the failure to provide the promised depot. In response, the Santa Fe in the autumn of 1902, fitted up an old railroad car next to the beet dump and installed a former teacher and local editor as station agent at thirty dollars a month, soon to be upped to fifty dollars. At best, this was a temporary expedient, and colonists had to fight for a permanent station. In the summer of 1902, the Salvation Army had contributed $500 and the colonists would subscribe a like amount.[50] Two years passed. Late in 1904, when the building contract had been let but no work done, the *Amity Optimist* echoed the common complaint.

> *Seasons coming! Seasons going!*
> *And we're growing old, slack!*
> *While we all are shiv'ring, swelt'ring,*
> *In that same old dingy shack.*

And we wonder what's the reason,
While the railroad has the "mon.,"
They don't get a hustle on them
And soon get the depot done.[51]

When Booth-Tucker made the circuit of the farm colonies in the spring and summer of 1899, he was "very pleased at the progress made," especially at Amity, where the Army "could easily locate 20,000 Salvationists." He also noted that every branch of agriculture was being taught the colonists "by experts," with even the children being trained.[52] This was a subject close to the Commander's heart. His colonists needed the best technical advice available. At one point in the summer of 1898, Booth-Tucker contemplated selecting "either a soldier or an officer to go through the regular course at one of our best Agricultural Colleges," but also with some work at another school where irrigation was practiced. Requesting Army Secretary Holz to investigate costs and dates of enrollment, Booth-Tucker added a postscript: "It ought to be someone who has some elementary and practical knowledge of farming. We don't want a mere *theorist*, or scientist!"[53]

Apparently nothing came of this idea, but it is clear that the Army believed in tapping farm experts whenever possible. At Amity, leaders invited the state agricultural college at Fort Collins to conduct institutes, generally in February of each year. They were quick to call upon the college in special situations: the 1902 Blackleg epidemic, the 1903 alfalfa malady, and the poisoning of a number of cattle in 1905. When salts built up in the soil, again in 1905, they called in the Colorado State Engineer for consultation.[54]

Fort Collins professors sometimes used as a sounding board the Amity Institute, a local self-improvement group sometimes called the Farmers' Institute. It began in October 1898 when William Wiley spoke to colonists about his hopes for Amity and several old-timers discussed their experiences at the Union Colony in Greeley. A week or two later, at a social affair at colonist Robert Newman's house, settlers listened to talks on the Sooner rush into Indian Territory and the work of the Salvation Army in Denver, then organized the Amity Institute to combine sociability and individual betterment. It sought museum specimens, developed a library, and held discourses on books, travel or popular science. At its meetings, colonists enjoyed refreshments and gossip, heard recitations and listened to music performed by fellow settlers.[55]

Most of all, though, the Amity Institute became a forum for discussion of agricultural problems at the colony. It maintained a collection of farming materials, as well as "a magnificent supply of Salvation Army literature." It was to the Institute that Booth-Tucker spoke on improving farm techniques. It was there that several irrigation experts, including the Indian Pagertee, discussed water problems, and a visiting major from Utah gave settlers the benefit of his expertise on poultry raising. Members welcomed such outsiders, for they used the Institute as a public meeting for the exchange of ideas. When they decided to act on an idea, the Institute became the means of implementing it. Here they elected the creamery directors, the board of water commissioners, or even the committee to plan the annual Fourth of July celebration.[56]

It was through the Institute, too, that the Army conducted its annual "Gala Days." These were autumn competitions at which judges (generally colony officers) awarded money prizes for the best crops and livestock.[57] These competitions were distinct from the yearly Harvest Home Festival—a fund-raising enterprise which also exhibited the colonists' work. The Harvest Home Festival was a nation-wide affair at which goods and produce contributed by farmers were auctioned off with the proceeds going to the Army.[58]

The role of the colony manager in providing practical advice and example was considered the key to colony success. The first manager, the versatile and energetic Thomas Holland, who also served as National Colonization Secretary, moved in and out of Fort Amity where he was in charge four different times.[59]

His role varied. In his dual capacity as Colonization Secretary and time-to-time supervisor of the Amity settlement, he was involved in publicity, fund-raising, and day-to-day activity, once even serving as executor for the estate of deceased settler William Carter. When making local decisions, he more than once sought the assistance of the Army Board of Trustees or the Finance Council in New York. He took a firm position with respect to the ouster of E. D. Cox, who had defaulted on his payments, moved off the land but refused to give up the place. Holland asked officials in New York to make the formal decision. In another instance, he had agreed to help an Amity colonist underwrite a new warehouse to replace one destroyed by fire, but when he found that private capital was available, he asked National Headquarters to nullify the commitment. "It is necessary for the manager to be on good terms with the people, if possible," he explained.[60]

Because of the burden of national duties, Holland was replaced by Brigadier Joseph Streeton in the fall of 1899. In "a pair of corduroy riding breeches, long cavalry boots, fustian coat and vest and white slouched hat," a bronzed and ruddy Streeton cut an impressive figure astride a bronco. He was at once postmaster, notary public, master gardener, "and as daring a horseman as one would desire to see." His wife, Marsha, milked, churned, and raised chickens in addition to

rearing children; and the home farm, under Streeton's touch was
regarded as "an object lesson on the colony."[61] Within a year, Streeton
was replaced by Brigadier Henry Stillwell, one of the British pioneers
in Salvation Army work on the Pacific Coast, and Stillwell, in turn, gave
way to Holland again in 1902. After Holland's severe injury in 1903,
Staff Captain James H. Durand was in charge for a time, although
Holland retained as close ties as his health permitted. And after he left
Fort Romie in the spring of 1906, Nels Erikson returned as manager of
the Colorado settlement. How long he remained is not clear.[62]

If colonists looked to the manager for guidance, they also looked to
his aide-de-camp, the lesser officer whose job it was to handle many of
the day-to-day problems, especially farm-connected problems. Ensign
Nels Erikson performed that function at the beginning of Amity;
subsequently the role was filled by Staff Captain William French, who
arrived in the autumn of 1898. How the settlers came to view French
was indicated in a piece from the *Amity Optimist* in 1904:

> *If your drag's out of order; your harrow won't work;*
> *And your discer gets broke on a clod —*
> *The plow which you'd reckoned would do all your work*
> *Won't so much as turn over a sod —*
> *Your shovel is loaned and your best hoe is lost,*
> *And you can't even find a monkey wrench;*
> *Why, then is the time to get up and howl,*
> *And take all your troubles to Staff Captain French.*[63]

Given the opportunity (and frequently some subsidy from the
Salvation Army), a number of colonists quickly branched out from
agriculture to become small-town businessmen as the community took
shape. Already in mid-1899, Commander Booth-Tucker was boasting
about the Amity townsite, which he valued at $100,000 "although it
only costs us about $7,000." By the summer of 1902, Amity was de-
scribed as a "thriving community" of red roofs with all the amenities of
a well-established village. A number of its buildings, including homes,
were made of stone from a nearby quarry developed by colonist Frank
McAbee, a former grocery clerk from Alliance, Ohio, who received
loans for quarry equipment as he built up a business estimated to be
worth $2,000.[64] One stone structure was a livery stable, owned by
George H. Thomas, one of the Chicago pioneers who had once served
on the London Metropolitan Police Force and who was considered
"one of the hardest workers on the colony." In 1901, Thomas had
acquired a new hay mower and rake and was doing contract work.
During the next year, he outfitted another building as a meat market;
and when Rider Haggard visited the town in 1905, Thomas was still

Inauguration of the Salvation Army Colony in California, done in color by Manuel Valencia for the Western *War Cry*. (From the John E. T. Milsaps Scrapbook, vol. 1, Houston Metropolitan Research Center, Houston Public Library)

Salvation Army officers and colony supporters who officially opened
Fort Romie. Photographed January 6, 1898, at Paraiso Springs by Man-
uel Valencia. Booth-Tucker is seated third from the right; Wallace Win-
chell (fourth from the left) and John Milsaps (extreme right), standing.
(From the John E. T. Milsaps Scrapbook, vol. 2, Houston Metropolitan
Research Center, Houston Public Library)

MAMMOTH SALVATION ARMY
SOCIAL DEMONSTRATIONS
CONDUCTED BY

EW YEAR'S NIGHT,

Saturday, January 1st,

ECHANICS'

AVILION,

GREAT

EW YEAR'S TREE

for Poor Children and an

ld=fashioned

BARBECUE

FOR 5,000 PEOPLE.

ayor Phelan presides.

Commander Booth-Tucker.

TUESDAY NIGHT,

JANUARY 4th,

Golden Gate Hall,

625 SUTTER STREET,

LAUNCHING
OF
THE

Soledad Colony

And Installation of the

FIRST 150 COLONISTS

RABBI DR. VOORSANGER presides,
Assisted by the

Citizens' Colonization
Committee.

COMMANDER BOOTH=TUCKER.

Poster announcing the launching of the Fort Romie colony and fund-raising meeting in San Francisco, 1898. (Poster 184, Drawer 6, Poster Collection, Houston Metropolitan Research Center, Houston Public Library)

·WILLIAM·BOOTH· General

·F. and E. BOOTH·TUCKER· in Command of the U.S?

War Cry

THE·WORLD·FOR·GOD

of the Salvation Army

An Official Gazette Pacific Coast Division

No. 665.

San Francisco, Saturday, August 25, 1900.

Price 5 Cents.

THE MAN BEHIND THE PLOW.——(See Page 2.)

Commander Booth-Tucker, "The Man Behind the Plow," drawn by Manuel Valencia for the cover of *The War Cry* (SF), August 25, 1900. (Houston Metropolitan Research Center, Houston Public Library)

Colonist family and typical home, Fort Amity, Colorado. Stone for Amity's buildings came from colonist Frank McAbee's quarry. (Colorado Historical Society Library)

Grocery and dry-goods store in Amity, originally built by colonist James Childs. (Colorado Historical Society Library)

Amity, looking south on Washington Avenue. On the left, the schoolhouse dedicated in 1903. (Colorado Historical Society Library)

One of the larger frame houses in Amity.
(Colorado Historical Society Library)

Machine shop, Amity townsite. (Colorado Historical Society Library)

Broom shop, Amity, probably owned by Frank
McAbee. (Colorado Historical Society Library)

Amity farmers loading cantaloupes for shipment. (Colorado Historical Society Library)

Commander Booth-Tucker (fourth from the left) at a banquet during a visit to Amity in early 1903, with Adjutant Margaret W. Carter (holding the baby) and probably Joseph H. Hargreaves (extreme right). (Colorado Historical Society Library)

operating a farm and a grocery business and had just been elected sheriff of Prowers County at a salary of $1800 a year.[65]

Another of the original settlers, James H. Childs, a railway check clerk from Chicago, supported his wife and nine children with a retail business, which expanded from time to time, to become the largest general merchandise store in town; it, like Thomas's was underwritten by Army loans. In addition to an outright loan to purchase the building for Childs, the Army on two occasions took his promissory notes for $300 and $1,000 respectively on the security of his store and other buildings. In 1908, Childs opened a cotton-glove factory at Amity, which was then on the decline, and he soon moved the plant to Pueblo.[66]

James Burrows was colonist, Salvation Army officer, columnist for the *Holly Chieftain* and by 1902 "landlord of the Amity hotel." One of the original settlers, John H. Newman also opened a store and in the summer of 1902 bought out the hardware owned by William Carter, a Salvation Army officer who rented colony premises but was probably not a colonist himself. Carter also ran a soda fountain and candy store. By the summer of 1905, David Coker, one of the 1898 pioneers, was running a small restaurant and boarding house and had established a soda pop plant, the product of which he distributed to nearby towns.[67]

A number of blacksmiths came and went, including E. M. Cram who arrived in 1901 with "wife and eight robust chidren" and whose new triplets startled the colony the next year. Arthur Inman's barbershop was burned out shortly after it opened, but he continued outdoors with a second-hand chair. Carl Erikson ran a dairy farm but soon added a harness shop and a thriving coal business. A latecomer, James Pinkham, known as "a hustler," operated a feed and grain business with his own modern gasoline engine grinder. L. A. Doble, formerly a tinsmith, pursued a dual occupation as dairy farmer and as "the Amity tinner."[68]

When the new Bank of Amity was established with a capital of $5,000 in 1904 or 1905, A. J. Davy, the irrigation expert of 1898, was named manager. Whether this was the old agricultural credit association, based on the Raiffeisen model of Germany that Booth-Tucker thought in 1903 had been the first of its kind established in the United States, is not clear. In any event, Davy was there on the afternoon of July 9, 1908, when Kid Wilson and Henry Starr robbed the bank of $1,100 and escaped into New Mexico.[69]

In good times, Amity was a bustling commercial center, catering to the needs of its rural population. The Salvation Army encouraged its diversity and often granted loans to help establish businesses or artisans. Just as it advanced funds for colonists' homes and livestock, it was willing to provide money for blacksmith tools, for repairing Inman's barber shop after the fire, for "moving and remodeling Butcher Shop," or for "Purchase of Store building for Childs." In several instances, its officers helped locate vacant buildings across the Kansas line at Tribune or Coolidge and subsidized their movement to the Amity townsite.[70] It was clear to numerous visitors that Amity was indeed a thriving economic hub for several hundred people, and by 1902 it was also "becoming an intellectual, as well as a moral and religious, center for the countryside at large."[71]

Among the typically small-town institutions, the Amity Institute was probably stronger than most because of the encouragement of Salvation Army officers and the compactness of the colony, which made for a lively and orderly social life. Early in 1901, a literary society was organized to meet regularly and to enjoy, among other events, the music of the Holly orchestra and a debate on the question: "Who was the greatest General, Grant or Lee?" Lee won. A sewing circle for the benefit of the Cherry Tree Home for orphans provided an outlet for the ladies, but all colonists were invited to combine their sense of history with festivity and celebrate on April 18 the anniversary of the original location with Old Settlers' Day.[72]

Beginning in May 1902, the colony had a folksy weekly newspaper, *The Amity Sentinel*, published by A. F. Glase on a second-hand press bought with funds subscribed by the Army and by local residents. A former schoolteacher, Glase subsequently became agent at the new Amity railroad station and sold his interest to a man named Brakeman, who in September 1903 rolled the first issue of the renamed *Amity Optimist* off the press. The *Optimist* was described as "a spicy paper, with a clever editor who has a weakness for poetry" which included much on the colony "dished up in a very interesting way." In 1905, John Dautrich of Rocky Ford assumed the helm, but mysteriously disappeared, after which owner-editor Stewart Lewis made a short-lived effort to publish the *Amity Observer*.[73] Unfortunately copies of none of these three papers seem to have survived.

With the Salvation Army's emphasis on family and with the compact physical layout of farms and homes, it is not surprising that the schoolhouse became the center of community social life, nor that the Army would pay considerable attention to the colony's children, of whom there were about fifty as of July 1898. The Army took the lead in arranging the organization of a new school district and by October classes were being held on the upper floor of the colony office with at least one teacher.[74] At the same time, with county funds, during the winter the colonists built a new stone schoolhouse, which, according to Booth-Tucker, "acts also as a barracks for our meetings, and Headquarters for the Farmers Institute." The structure was officially dedicated on Washington's Birthday, 1899. At a meeting of the school

board on May 1, Colonel Holland was elected President, a special
school tax of fifteen mills was voted, and it was announced that there
were forty-two school-age children.[75] Centrally located, the school
building became the focal point for community activity, but it was soon
outgrown. Rather than add a second story, the colonists constructed a
second schoolhouse, completed earlier but dedicated in 1903 by the
Commander, who reported that with four teachers and 140 students,
the schools were already overcrowded.[76]

Given the militancy of the Salvation Army and the place of music in
its activities, it is not astonishing that recreational, educational, and
religious patterns at Amity should reflect conventional Army attitudes.
Spokesmen for the Army were quick to point out that all of the colonies
were nonsectarian and without religious qualification. Colonists were
not required to be "soldiers" in the Salvation Army; other denominations were represented and some drove to Holly for Sunday church
services rather than attend the Army's meetings.[77] The absence of
alcohol and dance halls was the direct result of Salvation Army policy;
yet this was but a beginning, according to the editor of *All the World*,
writing from the vantage point of London in 1900. "The sunny skies of
Italy can scarcely rival the sunshine of Colorado," he said, but freedom
from "the baneful influences of public-house life . . . does not entirely
free us from the contaminating influences of sin, so that a soldiers
armour is needed at Amity, as elsewhere."[78]

The Army took care to provide that "soldiers armour" and to keep
it obvious to the colonists. Not only was the Corps active locally, but its
members also traveled to other portions of the state to spread the
Gospel with music, marching, and open-air meetings. There was a
surprising number of Army officers in the settlement, either as ad-
ministrators or as colonists; and their active religion was clearly the
focal point of Fort Amity life. Booth-Tucker in 1902 found the spiritual
side of colonization "most encouraging." Conversions were common
and at Amity about one hundred children were members of the Junior
Company and some seventy Soldiers were on the Roll.[79] Every social
occasion was an opportunity for a musical or religious meeting—
preferably a combination of the two.

Even when friends helped Ben Winchester celebrate his twenty-
fourth birthday in October 1898 with a dinner and a social hour spiced
with organ and cornet music, the affair "finished up with a good
Salvation meeting." Also typical was the Army's "battle of song," waged
in the schoolhouse early in March of the following year. Primarily for
the young, it involved an hour-and-a-half of song and chorus, followed
by "a good prayer meeting," led by Ensign Wallace Davy.[80] As manager
and ranking Salvationist officer, Thomas Holland held special sessions
with the Soldiers to discuss such topics as "how we can make our

meetings more impressive and profitable." He usually led the Sunday evening meetings, sometimes with large audiences which included a number of cowboys who "evidently enjoyed the lively singing and earnest talking of the Army Soldiers." And often Holland had the assistance of the Junior String Band, organized by David Coker, or of Mrs. William Stevens singing "a beautiful solo of her own composition," before the Colonel "finished up with a stirring appeal to the unconverted."[81]

Joseph Streeton continued the tradition, holding meeting after meeting among the colonists. During the week, one observer noted, Amity dress was western-style cowboy hats, overalls, and shirt-sleeves, but on Sunday out came the formal Salvation Army uniforms: "Brigadier Streeton's familiar form rises to give out 'Shout aloud Salvation, Boys!' The string band starts, the piano, cornet and fiddle chime in, the crowd sings, and you fancy yourself in Heaven."[82] Every visiting officer, from the auditor who came to inspect the books, to the brother of one of the colonists, was called upon to conduct services or to describe missionary or other church work. Included was one of the Army's genuine eccentrics, "Joe the Turk," a huge Armenian Salvationist who appeared in Turkish fez, crimson jacket, and pantaloons and with his ink pad and stamp left the motto "Jesus Saves" on walls, linens, and furniture wherever he went. In addition, at Amity, he demonstrated his musical talents and gave a detailed account of his own conversion.[83]

No persons were more active in this regard than Frederick and Emma Booth-Tucker, both of whom visited Fort Amity a number of times and invariably conducted a rousing meeting, as the Commander did in the summer of 1899. Both were back the following spring for four days of revivalism, and a year later the Consul returned for a brief but busy stay. Under a banner "United for God and the Army," she presided at the wedding of Nels Erikson and Fredericka Rupp. The Consul addressed the youth of the colony, and presented each child over the age of five with a bank book with one dollar to its credit. She dedicated five babies, "in her own motherly, tender way," laid the cornerstone of the new Cherry Tree orphanage and planted some walnut seeds nearby. Somewhere in this full schedule she found time for a banquet, a musical program, and the inevitable religious meeting. It was at Fort Amity two years later that Emma Booth-Tucker "conducted her last meeting on earth, during which some forty-six souls knelt at the mercy seat." Enroute back to Chicago, she was killed in a train accident in which Colonel Holland also was severely injured.[84]

The Commander had been at the colony twice in 1903, once in the spring when he helped celebrate the fifth anniversary of the settlement, dedicated the schoolhouse, and addressed "a huge concourse of people." "About 200 buggies & 1000 present," he recorded in his diary. On the following evening, he ended his visit with a hard-fought religious meeting, where "the soldiers made a splendid dash for souls," and the Commander himself did well in the "hand-to-hand conflict." After his wife's death, the shattered Booth-Tucker paid a farewell visit to Amity before leaving the country. In what was one of his last appearances in the United States, he was sent on his way with the singing of a farewell poem from the *Optimist* and a final rip-roaring revival meeting in the stone schoolhouse.[85]

Another concrete example of the Salvation Army's mission in Colorado was the establishment of the Cherry Tree Home. Late in 1900, the Army had decided to move this orphanage from its cramped quarters in Rutherford, New Jersey, to "the glorious wide-open of God's prairies" at Amity.[86] Construction was finished late in 1901 at a cost of roughly $20,000, and the Home was described as "a beautiful, palacelike building," one of the finest in the area. Built of stone, largely by colonist labor, the two-story structure had full attic and basement and was 100 feet long and 45 feet wide in the wings. It featured gas heating, hot and cold running water, and porcelain bathtubs, with water supplied by a large windmill; it had thirty-three rooms, with dining facilities, kitchen, and offices on the first floor and separate laundry building.[87]

Under the charge of Captain Alice Benjamin from thirty to fifty children—a "bright looking lot"—were transferred from New Jersey, their transportation provided free by the Santa Fe Railroad Company. At peak, the Home housed sixty children between the ages of three and eighteen, drawn from nearly a dozen states, including Colorado. Captain Benjamin soon relinquished management, and her place was taken by Staff Captain Joseph H. Hargreaves and his wife. When visited by the secretary of the Colorado State Board of Charities and Corrections in 1903, Hargreaves was assisted by a staff of eight, including Clara Long, the teacher. A practical education, not adoption, was the end in mind. The orphans were to learn working skills—the actual tasks of gardening, farming, tree growing, and livestock care. As a local editor expressed it, "An ideal destiny is planned for the children—that of land owners on the colony as they reach maturity."[88]

But few, if any, reached maturity while at Amity. The Cherry Tree Home was never a complete success, whether because of the expense, the lack of nearby medical facilities, or perhaps the shock of the dry treeless landscape on eastern and urban children. Whatever the reason, when the Army was given a large estate at Lytton Springs, California, the inhabitants of the Cherry Tree Home were moved west, an advantage in that the State of California paid half their maintenance expense. Thus by 1905, the large, modern building at Amity was for the time being vacant.[89]

This presented an opportunity for the Salvation Army to experiment with another of Booth-Tucker's favorite schemes. When the Commander passed through Kansas City for the opening of the Cherry Tree Home in 1901, he talked to reporters about the establishment of a tuberculosis sanitarium for the poor. He envisioned a building large enough for 1,000 beds, a place, he said, where the sick and needy could "come live with us, and for $3.00 or $4.00 a week obtain medicine, good food and bracing air." When cured, they graduated to a cottage and ten acres. At a rate of $4 a week, the institutional income would total $4,000. Of this, colonists were to receive $2,000 in exchange for their eggs, vegetables, and other products; $1,000 would defray the other operating expenses; and the remaining $1,000 would be added to the general colony treasury for the assistance of the settlers.[90]

After the untimely death of Consul Booth-Tucker in 1903, the Santa Fe Railroad Company gave as a memorial $10,000, with which the Commander established the Emma Booth-Tucker Sanitarium at the old Cherry Tree Home. It was hardly on the scale he had outlined in Kansas City, but it was a beginning. According to advertisements, for $25 a month "and up," including board, room, medicine, and medical attention, tuberculosis would be treated using Dr. David Wark's new methods, under his direct supervision. Dr. William S. Greenard, who also owned a farm at the colony but was not a colonist as such, was in charge in 1905 and reported the sanitarium doing well. Patients did come from various parts of the country, but few were able to pay even limited expenses and the establishment closed down in 1906. It soon re-opened as a private hospital, but its doors were permanently shut by the end of August 1907, and several schemes by other groups to acquire the building never materialized. By this time, the Army was in the process of liquidating its holdings at the colony, but the old Cherry Tree Home stood abandoned for years before it was finally torn down. The Army's records in 1917 showed that $24,731.75 had gone into it.[91]

Although the presence of the Salvation Army and the status of the colony as an experiment made Amity something less than a representative, rural American town, the scarcity of information makes it difficult to reconstruct a profile of the average Amity colonist. According to the Census of 1900, the average age of twenty-eight heads of families there was 37.8 years. That excluded Streeton, the manager, but included five renters, without whom the average head of household age was 39. Except for Elizabeth Slaymaker, a twenty-five-year-old widow with three small children, and William Redrich (or Reddick), a Canadian-born widower, who lived under the same roof with his Norwegian servant, Annie Jacobs, all colonists were male and all were married. Twenty-six heads of households (widow and widower excluded) had been married on the average 14.23 years; not counting the renters, the figure was 16 years. Twenty-eight heads, including two with no children then living with them, had an average of 3.5 children, higher than the national level. Without the renters, the average was 4 children at home; without the older people whose children were grown, the average rose to 4.38.

Of the Amity heads of families, thirteen (46 percent) were foreign-born. Of these, six (21.4 percent of the total) had been born in England, four in Canada, and one each in Sweden, Germany, and Ireland. Of the fifteen colonist heads born in the United States as of 1900, five had been born in Illinois, two each in Ohio and Missouri, and one each in Kentucky, Kansas, Pennsylvania, Maine, New Jersey, and New York. So far as can be ascertained, three had lived in Kansas immediately before moving to Amity; possibly two came directly from Canada; one each from Ohio, California, Nebraska, and Missouri, while the previous residence of one is unknown. But thirteen (46 percent) had moved directly from Illinois. Although Commander Booth-Tucker sometimes labeled them "residents of the New York slums," visitors referred to the colony as "Little Chicago," and one settler is supposed to have observed that "this is just like a suburb of Chicago."[92] After 1902 or 1903, a larger percentage of new colonists tended to come from such states as Kansas, Iowa, Missouri, or the Indian Territory, with a smattering of easterners thrown in. Illinois was no longer the major source.

The census of 1900 does not give prior occupations. Of those interviewed by H. Rider Haggard in 1905, four did not mention their work before becoming colonists but the others represented a wide spectrum. Apart from the local corps, five were Salvation Army officers: Joseph Hargreaves, John Davy, William L. Stevens, James Burrows, and Augustus Priebe. Others, like A. K. Durand, son of Staff Captain James Durand, who for a time was colony manager, and Frank McAbee, brother of an officer in Denver, were related to Salvation Army personnel.[93] Hargreaves and Stevens both came because of health problems, and the Army sent a number of other officers as part of the Amity Corps in the hope that Colorado's dry climate would have a convalescent effect upon them.[94]

Of Haggard's 1905 group, three had previously been carpenters, including George Nicol and the father-son combination, Robert and John Newman—all from Chicago. Frank McAbee of Alliance, Ohio, George Waidner of Baltimore and J. A. Ziegler of Sioux City had all worked in the grocery business; McAbee and Waidener had to borrow money to come; Ziegler had close to $100 when he came to visit his father, liked Amity and stayed on. Erik Erickson and Charles E. Gaylord had both been Chicago streetcar conductors: Erikson brought $25 in capital; Gaylord came with nothing but a family and a good education—three years of medical school.[95]

Charles Barkman had been a butter and cheese salesman in Kansas City. He disliked the town and his earnings netted him no savings. James H. Childs had been a clerk for the Chicago & Alton Railway. Carl Erikson had barely made ends meet as a tailor in the same town; L. A. Doble, the Sioux City tinsmith, had $10 in his pocket when he reached Amity; English-born David Coker, a painter from Chicago, arrived with $13 and four children. William Sachtler had been an iron moulder in Norwalk, Connecticut, while W. J. Grindrod had been a packing house worker in St. Joseph, Missouri. Among the original settlers, Walter Baldwin had been a brick mason in Chicago; another, unnamed, had learned shoemaking in that same city, where he had drifted after losing "valuable mill and elevator property in Iowa." Thomas Cloughley had been an "engineer," a loose generic term at the turn of the century, making $17.50 a week, and had saved about $800 when he left Omaha in 1905, a move prompted mainly by his wife's poor health and a desire for a better place in which to bring up five children.[96]

How much agricultural experience there was in the background of many of these settlers is difficult to say. At least five of those surveyed by Haggard had previously been farmers, generally in Kansas, Oklahoma, or Colorado. H. W. Manning had done poorly at Alamosa, a hundred miles or so to the west, in part because of sickness. Benjamin Morris had farmed but failed to obtain a homestead when Indian Territory opened. From the sale of his Kansas farmland, Charles Stimson came with $1,000 in hand and was the first to obtain title at Amity. S. A. Inman had farmed in northeast Kansas, but arrived in Colorado with no capital and only a few head of livestock. "Pace-setter" Louis H. Kephart, brought in to encourage sheep raising, was familiar with ranching in the Southwest and apparently had some funds of his own. Others, among them Robert Newman, had been raised on farms but were not necessarily familiar with irrigated cultivation, although one Kansas farmboy no doubt was: Elmer Harris had left his father's farm to do some freighting in the Rockies and was so intrigued with the colony as he passed through that he took up an allotment and stayed.[97] Salvation Army officer Gus Priebe had earlier done general gardening work in Ohio; O. M. Pringle, a land agent in Oklahoma, came with considerable prior experience in growing fruits and vegetables.[98]

On the other hand, the basic premise of the colonization experiments was that the country was uplifting; even without a rural upbringing or extensive farm expertise at the beginning, with proper direction, any honest, industrious man could till the soil with profit. Neophytes learned quickly. One of the most successful at Amity, according to Booth-Tucker, had never been out of New York City before: "He had a little one-horse express wagon on the East Side; but he took to farming as a duck takes to water, and he walks off with a large share of our prizes."[99]

Even so, irrigated farming brought its own inherent problems. By 1905, when H. Rider Haggard was lauding the virtues of the Army's American colonies and the Army was pushing its larger settlement scheme before Parliament in London, Fort Amity was falling upon evil days. For several years annual crop yields had dropped season by season. Land that once produced twenty tons of sugar beets or two-and-a-half tons of alfalfa per acre per season came to yield practically nothing. Orchards withered and crops failed; even some of the building foundations began to disintegrate. The problem was a salt build-up in the soil, erroneously referred to at the colony as alkali. Originally, Colonel Holland had consulted a committee of "successful farmers and fruit growers" about the Amity site, which met their approval. But, as Holland explained later, in order to obtain superior water rights on the Buffalo Creek Canal, he had chosen bottom land, "which unfortunately has proved to be lacking in natural drainage." The result, he said: "Irrigation of the higher lands North of the Colony has caused the *more* or *less* water logging, and the *more* or *less* alkaling of our low-lying land amounting in round figures to some six hundred acres."[100]

Holland and the colonists had read government bulletins and had consulted "the two best Engineers in that part of the country." Late in 1904, when the saline problem had become acute, the Army called in Antoine Jacobs, a civil engineer. On his advice, a drainage ditch was dug and some tile laid, but conditions were not improved. When the Colorado State Engineer was consulted in 1905, he advised deeper drainage and additional tile. Jacobs concurred: along with an enlarged drainage channel, he recommended laying 30,000 feet of tile, to cost an estimated $16 to $20 per acre.[101]

Holland believed that proper drainage might run as much as $30 an acre, but conceded that outlays might be less should tiling the lower land draw water off the higher land and make further tiling unnecessary. In any event, he considered it "our only salvation," an investment to prevent "the destruction of a large part of the colony land." Should the situation worsen, the Army might find itself with "an alkali swamp incapable of producing even the commonest weeds."[102]

Holland incorporated these assessments and more into a bleak report which prompted a special meeting of the Salvation Army Board of Trustees in March 1906. What was most disconcerting, according to him, was that from the beginning the colonists had not been able to support their families on twenty acres and meet their rental, interest, and other obligations without Army aid or outside employment. Even those on higher, better-drained ground had not been able to make ends meet. Now came the crushing blow of excess salinity, despite reliance on expert opinions in making the original land selection. Over six hundred acres required tiling, Holland said, at a cost he now judged might go as high as $50 an acre. Added to these "discouraging and heart-breaking features" was the fact that two of the four horses bought for drainage ditching had died and the others were in poor shape. Faced with these "appalling facts," the trustees agonized but finally agreed to expend $5,000 in tiling the worst land, but made it clear that they regarded this as "a forlorn hope," "a last endeavor." While praising Holland for "the up-hill fight and self-denials that he had made for and on behalf of the Colony," the Board begrudgingly authorized going ahead, but stipulated that as much of the drainage work as possible should be done by the colonists themselves and deducted from their debts to the Army. To raise funds, a colony appeal was to be made, with a copy of Holland's depressing report accompanying each appeal.[103]

Chief Secretary Hicks passed the trustees' decision on to Holland in a letter which underscored the high-level opposition to further expenditures for drainage and brought an explanatory and defensive response from the Colonel.[104] A few months later the Army's Finance Council expedited the trustees' approval, when it earmarked $5,000 for "Reclamation work on Amity lands, including machinery and equipment." Even more disconcerting was another item endorsed by the Council at the same time: "Maintenance of Colonists for one year," $1,000.[105]

Even before the Council's formal endorsement, carloads of tile were arriving and a large ditching machine was at work at Amity. Much of the tiling had been completed by early 1907, but none was to be done on the west side of the colony until the rest of the land that had been drained or was to be drained was satisfactorily occupied or disposed of.[106]

Despite optimistic reports, the saline problem was not easily solved. Planting and irrigation proceeded, but the land would not produce. The drifting away of settlers increased: a dribble became an exodus, and when the Army Finance Council met in a three-day session late in January 1907, it was clear that Fort Amity was foundering. The council brought forth some tough recommendations: "Retrenchment in the expense of management." The postmistress and two hired hands on the home farm were to go; Army cattle were to be sold; and with the moving from Amity of the National Colonization Office, sharp reductions were to be made in expense of postage, stationery, and telegrams. Loans were authorized for colonists up to $500, with crops as security. Renters and colonists who worked away from their land were under a strict injunction to pay their monthly rental fee on time and to dispose of surplus livestock immediately. Nels Erikson proposed that the Army itself farm 320 acres of the best land "so as to demonstrate its possibilities," but the Council rejected the idea, arguing that colonists on their own land provided a better testimony, and it authorized Erikson to rent unoccupied lands as best he could—even for nominal fees if working the soil might reduce the saline content. The Council also supported the idea of a sugar beet factory on Army land, a concept which never went beyond the discussion stage.[107]

Meanwhile, the Army had large outlays, including its annual payment of $2,856.82 to the Arkansas Valley Sugar Beet & Irrigated Land Company. It continued its $100 subscription to the Cantaloupe Association and added more to pay for melon losses. To expenses of 1908, the Army contributed $500 for "Leveling Land," another $500 for completing the tiling system, and $1,000 for "putting Main Drains down to the Grade," not to mention another $300 for seeds.[108]

As colonists withdrew, the Army made settlements with them to take improvements into account. The general policy was to pay the settler for his improvements, which might range from $35 to $250, then resettle a new colonist, or if that proved impossible, as it did after 1905, to rent the property. At the same time the colony fell into the doldrums, the Army found itself paying taxes on a number of tracts that had reverted to it when settlers left.[109]

That settlement payments to colonists were generally relatively small indicates that the debts owed to the Army were large. Settlers did not reduce their indebtedness, and the Army made no real effort to enforce contracts. Indeed, the manager of the colony in 1905 reported that a number of the new settlers had refused to sign contracts and that affairs were so muddled he could not be certain who had signed and who had not. Recognizing this confusion, Booth-Tucker on his last trip to Fort Amity had promised a relaxing of fiscal demands and an extension of contracts over a twenty-year period—this, he said, "in consideration of the difficulties experienced up to date, and the tangled web into which the colonists accounts had got. . . ."[110]

In New York, the Army's hard-nosed legal consul Ferris found these arguments convincing. "We cannot afford to fire them off the Colony, we cannot afford to press the screws too hard, now that we have them: and we cannot get over the fact that we are their Moses and must bring them safely through their difficulties onto the promised land, with a good unencumbered title." Still, he argued, the Army's investment had been secured and colonists required to fulfill their commitments.[111]

One historian of the colony reports that in 1907 or 1908 a Holly real-estate developer bought the Army's holdings "almost in its entirety, and the colony was abandoned," with the Army aiding the settlers "in transporting their families and goods to any desired location, and in securing employment."[112] Early in 1909 local newspapers spoke of a "Gigantic Land Deal," in which Joseph McMurtry and John G. Christopher, both of Holly, were to acquire the Amity townsite, including a number of businesses, and take an option on 2,000 adjacent acres at a total price of $250,000. The new owners were to bring in small industry and develop the farmland.[113] This ambitious plan failed to materialize, although McMurtry and Christopher did indeed purchase part of the colony property in 1909 and in 1912 and also dickered with the Army over oil rights; the total however, probably did not run to more than 340 acres, valued at $15,570.[114]

By 1909, Fort Amity had run its course: it had gone from robust expectation and seeming prosperity to decline and finally disintegration. From that time on, its history became one of dispersal of settlers and of disposition by the Army of fragments of property amidst the tidying up of its records.[115] If the expensive drainage system served its purpose in restoring the land to its former fertility, as ardent champions insisted, the improvement came too late to save the colonial experiment.[116]

CHAPTER SIX

Fort Herrick, Ohio

*. . . It is seldom that the Army has a chance to be
surrounded with the influence to enable it to take advantage
of so much success for the future, as at present surrounds
this Colony in Cleveland.*[1]

LOCATED NEAR WILLOUGHBY, OHIO, twenty miles from Cleveland and
not far from James A. Garfield's early home at Mentor, the Army's
third American farm colony, Fort Herrick, was established in the
summer of 1898 on land acquired from Myron T. Herrick and his
brother-in-law, James Parmalee, both important political and financial
figures in the state. It was Herrick, a future governor of Ohio, who first
introduced Booth-Tucker to Mark Hanna, master politician and
staunch friend of the Salvation Army. It was Hanna who took the
initiative in the campaign to raise $20,000 to finance the colony.[2]

A writer for *The War Cry* described Fort Herrick as "a beautiful
sweep of level land, fringed with a second growth of wood on its
western boundary and containing about 288 acres." Its cost was given
as from $25,000 to $30,000, although the property was carried on the
record books in 1901 at $14,400—the total price colonists would be
expected to pay.[3] Army officials were dickering for the land in May of
1898, when both Herrick and Parmalee visited National Headquarters
in New York. There, the legal advisor, Madison Ferris, passed on to his

colleagues the admonition of Parmalee that the Ohio settlement must be conducted "on thoroughly business lines." Always keep in mind, Ferris reiterated, "that the eyes of Cleveland are upon us; and not only that, but that everyone as they pass by Mentor, always are seeking out the residence of General Garfield, and, of course, cannot help but see our colony at the same time." ". . . Make this a little something extra," Ferris urged; make it "a model farm that will not only be a credit to us, but that will establish us in the hearts of these conservative people." Make it "a monument to the Salvation Army, that the world will admire." Booth-Tucker was perhaps more modest in his aspirations. He saw an opportunity to make Fort Herrick "a model institution of the kind and an important training ground for the colonies in the West."[4]

Ferris also advocated the selection of a superintendent "who will be both a godly person and of broad mind enough to overcome, properly, all the difficulties that may arise, and to carry out many details that will devolve upon us in this great work, in a business-like capacity." Here was an opportunity to impress Clevelanders, who, once stirred, might then support other Salvation Army endeavors.[5]

The man selected to head the colony was Adjutant Charles W. Bourne, a twenty-nine-year-old English-born Salvationist who had arrived in America in 1887. Booth-Tucker also designated Colonel Richard Holz, the National Social Secretary, to give broad oversight to the operation, at least until Thomas Holland was free to move to New York. Holz demurred, pleading overwork, and suggested that Bourne be given a brief outline of duties and policy, with monthly inspections by Holland or other officers; but Booth-Tucker stood firm, at least in 1898. By the middle of June, the Commander had established a Colonization Finance Council, to meet weekly, with Holz as a member.[6]

Adjutant Bourne established himself and family in the old house on the Fort Herrick grounds. The first male colonists were housed in a large barn; their families were to come later when cottages were finished. Construction proceeded in the summer of 1898 with Rogers, the Army architect, supervising. Holz had recommended renovation of the old house, but investigation showed it was not worth any investment over $75. Roger had drawn up plans for a new $500 house and office for Bourne, but the new Colonization Board vetoed the idea on the grounds of economy. By early September, when Fort Herrick colony was officially dedicated, eight cottages had been completed and families were moving in.[7]

Commander Booth-Tucker opened the colony formally with an impressive flag-raising ceremony attended by 2,000 people, according to *The War Cry*. It was a day of bands, processions, and oratory with one street being named Booth-Tucker Avenue and one speaker predicting that it would ultimately be lined with skyscrapers. In the evening, a religious meeting capped off the day, with fourteen souls saved.[8]

The opening was made with a handful of colonists, settled on much the same basis as those at Fort Romie and Fort Amity except that each settler received lesser amounts of land: each farmer was to get five to ten acres, each artisan, one to three acres, and in either case there was a ten-year lease with monthly payments ultimately leading to ownership. The sale of liquor was forbidden, and no manufacturing plant might be established without the Army's express consent.[9]

By Christmas Day 1898, the *New York Herald* could report that Fort Herrick now had ten families and that "the same order and earnestness of purpose obtain among them as in the two older colonies." This was a small-plot operation, with emphasis on such crops as potatoes, buckwheat, corn, and beans, and with close attention given to products which might have a local market. Like Hargreaves at Amity, one colonist, Fulton, who came from Woonsocket, Rhode Island, specialized in poultry. With two incubators and usually about 500 chicks in his brooders, he hatched eggs for nearby farmers, supplied the company store, and provided broilers to hotels in the area. One of the Harringtons was in charge of the colony "dairy," a limited operation where cream was separated, a small amount of butter made, and the surplus sold to neighbors. Later, Major McFee, also of the Army, was responsible for handling the ninety-five pairs of pigeons raised in the colony to provide squab for the local market and for the twenty-eight hives of bees which produced the honey and comb sold in the Fort Herrick store and in town. In addition, "cheery old Salvationists" ran a broom shop, using broom corn grown on colony land; and settlers' wives, under the eye of Mrs. Bourne, found a ready market locally for their jams, jellies, and other home-canned products.[10]

By the end of 1898, Fort Herrick had a post office, a schoolhouse, and a store. Earlier the Colonization Council had rejected a proposal of Bourne to stock a supply of hardware, advising him either to make arrangements with Cleveland hardware dealers or to persuade someone with a little capital to begin a store of his own. Soon Booth-Tucker could report that negotiations were under way for a store at the colony, from which the settlement would receive a commission on the sales. About the same time, George Cooke, a Cleveland Salvationist asked the Army to erect a cottage suitable for a loom with which to manufacture carpets. The Council agreed, permitting him to pay for it "in the usual way."[11]

When Richard Holz visited the colony in early 1899, he found only six families there, four of whom intended to move. Of the two who planned to remain, Ole Olson was a furniture upholsterer and repairer who was able to obtain a lot of work in the neighborhood; the other, Gus Priebe, "seemed to be the most cheerful of the whole lot." George Cooke, who was to start a Corps band at Herrick, planned to purchase five acres a mile away, with a better house. With Cooke, farming was secondary: carpet weaving was his main concern and living nearer town would help his business. Another family, the Arnolds, planned to move to a nearby farm as hired help; the Thorogoods contemplated returning to Cleveland, and Bennett, a pensioner, wished to remain as a tenant but not to buy his allotment.[12]

Holz, like Bourne, was optimistic but saw that there were problems. In areas near the wood several inches of water stood for days and ditches failed to drain the land properly. Because of this, the foundations of a number of cottages had settled, causing doors to stick, and, in the case of the Cookes, "putting the whole house out of joint." The rain poured through, "the chimney looked as if it might tumble off at any moment, and the roof was bent in." Although Ferris had earlier called for the construction of "proper houses," not the temporary "ramshackles" that had been thrown up at Amity, Holz found much discontent with the workmanship and the inferior grade of lumber used at Fort Herrick and recommended immediate repairs. He also proposed that the number of cottages be increased from nine to twelve, at a cost of from $3,000 to $3,500, and that the number of families be expanded to an even dozen for the season. Livestock and chickens were in excellent shape, seventy-five acres had been plowed, and Holz believed that "with proper manuring, good drainage, and intensive cultivation, it will become quite productive." But gravel for the road and drainage, perferably by tiling, seemed imperative.[13]

In visiting every colonist, Holz found "a good deal of grumbling and dissatisfaction," part of which he attributed to the fact that Bourne had held no religious services at Herrick for several months, though he regularly conducted one on Sundays at the Grange Hall two miles away. ". . . Naturally those who have been active soldiers have felt the lack of spiritual meetings very much," Holz remarked. He also observed low morale: colonists could not agree among themselves, and Bourne seemed unable to reconcile their differences and to keep matters from drifting.[14]

From the beginning there had been some question of Bourne's leadership. Apparently in response to queries by other officers, Booth-Tucker in July 1898 hoped that the colony would attract a "superior class of men" to run themselves without much supervision. He wondered if Priebe or Arnold might develop as settlers to a point where they could direct operations in which case Bourne could be sent elsewhere. As to the tendency of Bourne "to RUN THE COLONY AS AN

ORDINARY RANCH," said Booth-Tucker, "we shall have to watch the matter carefully and insist on our plan of action being carried out."[15]

It seems quite apparent that Bourne did not enjoy the kind of support from the Salvation Army Colonization Council that the other two colonies did. Numerous times he was overruled on financial matters and seemed unable to move, even in minor matters, without consultation. The Council agreed to allow Bourne to trade the Fort Herrick mare, valued at $35, for a horse worth $125, and throw in $25 cash, but by the time official approval was received, the horse had already been sold. The Council rejected Bourne's requisition for 100 bushels of oats, on the grounds that prices would be lower after harvest; in the meantime he should buy enough out of petty cash to tide the colony over. When Bourne presented a proposition from the Perkins Windmill Company to sink a well, erect a tank, windmill, and charcoal filtering plant for "less than $3,000," in order to remove impurities likely to cause "stone in the bladder," the Council vetoed the plan and deferred any alternative to a future meeting.[16]

Bourne's proposal to improve the colonists' cottages at a cost of $423.50 was disapproved and Consul Booth-Tucker was instructed to discuss matters with him "with a view to a more economical administration in the future." Subsequently, Bourne received permission from Holz, on behalf of the Council, to expend up to $50 on repair of settlers' housing. Bourne interpreted this to mean $50 for each cottage; the Council meant a total of $50 for all houses and took the occasion to admonish the manager "strongly to be more economical in his ideas and expenditures."[17]

The Council passed on all but the smallest expenditures at Fort Herrick—everything from putting a new floor in the horse barn to permission to subscribe to the Willoughby newspaper. Inasmuch as Bourne had to ask authorization to purchase two horses at $55 each, he also felt compelled to request that he be allowed to shoot a sick horse. Permission was granted and entered in the council minutes with a preface that was later lined out: "As in all probability the horse had died and been turned into sausage meat before the letter was read. . ."[18]

Although the need for economy seemed in the forefront, the Army poured a substantial amount of funds into the colony in the first year or two. Working with half of the $5,000 loan from Herrick and Parmalee, Bourne, by mid-July of 1898, even before the colony had opened, had spent nearly $2,400 on lumber, furniture, farm implements, livestock, contract plowing, seeding, and carpenters' wages, and the Council presented the loan notes for the second $2,500.[19] A typical colonist provided with house and farm buildings, loans for livestock, poultry, fertilizer, and seed might owe the Army from $700 to $800 in mid-1901, not counting land cost. As of June 28,1901, for example, Burt Harrington's account showed a debit of $711.50—$250.00 for house, $200.00 for barn, $50.00 for hog pen and chicken coop, and $211.50 to cover wagon, cultivator, harrow, team, pigs, two cows, and twenty-two chickens. W. F. Welk owed $805.00 at the same date. His debits included $375.00 for house, $400.00 for barn, plus $193.64 in loans and interest for cow, twenty-four chickens, sow, manure, and seed, but he had a credit of $63.00 in wages for work by members of his family.[20]

By September 28, 1900, apart from land, the Army's National Headquarters had put $13,707.97 into Fort Herrick. To the end of August, $925.36 of that had gone for livestock, including $4.75 for "ferrets." By July 23 of the following year, $829.23 had been spent on harness and farm implements and by September 16, 1901, $3,596.85 had gone into buildings and repairs, including $25.00 for "addition of a Gable on the Manager's Cottage."[21] Late in 1902, a water piping system, with windmill, was authorized at a cost of $1,370.00 One later source states that the colony experienced a number of disastrous crop failures until $9,000.00 was spent on tiling. Contemporary records and literature however reveal only token drainage tiling—$180.00 for five acres—and surface ditching, and it may be that Herrick has been confused with Amity. The colony showed little income of its own. Records for 1900 indicate that $4,273.60 came from national Headquarters of the Salvation Army and only $742.28 from sales of crops, pasture fees, work credit, and land rent payments, the latter totaling only $16.50.[22]

In early September 1902, after the colony's mailing address had been changed from Willoughby to Mentor, a correspondent for *The War Cry* visited Fort Herrick and wrote a romantic sketch, "A Day on the Colony," in which he noted that Bourne was still "governor" of the farm and that George Cooke, a former member of the "famous O.K. band" was still available to play the cornet at religious meetings. In fact, *The War Cry* commented, "nearly all of the colonists are now Salvation Army soldiers." Poultryman Fulton was still there, striving to meet hotel needs of a hundred broilers a week during the busy season and was also raising Belgian hares. Harrington's dairy operation was thriving, and records show that Charles Emory and W. F. Welk were still there, along with a number of new names—Hall and Reynolds and in 1903 Mason and Burgess.[23]

By October 1902, however, Major Joseph R. McFee seems to have replaced Bourne as manager. McFee wrote National Headquarters that purchase agreements were required for Fulton, Burt Harrington, Charles Emory, and that Bourne had sent the materials to New York but that they had never been completed and returned. As for the colonists in question, "They make the lack of agreement an excuse for not paying anything on the land," complained McFee, who also lamented that "the accounts are in a dreadful muddle. . . ." Ferris and Holland drew up the Fort Herrick agreement, in consultation with Bourne, and the legal advisor believed it to be a tight document. "I think this now carries everything that could possibly be needed or imagined for the next thousand years," Ferris commented.[24]

The number of colonists was never large—perhaps eight or nine families—and apparently some of those had left by late January 1903, when the Council discussed the question of whether to sell or retain on the home farm cattle that they had returned. A few months later, it authorized the expenditure of funds for horses and farm equipment for two new colonists. Later on, in the fall, a fire burned the barn and the hay in it, killing two horses and badly burning Major McFee on the head and foot as he saved one horse.[25]

Sometime late in 1903, just as the Consul began her last western tour, the Army decided to abandon the farm colony concept at Fort Herrick and to reorganize it as an "Industrial Colony," a drying-out home for inebriates. It became a "Farm for Growing Men as Well as Grain," a place for the "Salvage of Human Derelicts," as *The War Cry* put it.[26] This decision was likely prompted by an inability to expand because of high land prices around the settlement. Almost from the beginning—in 1899—colonists had asked more than the ten-acre maximum allotted to them, a request Booth-Tucker deferred for the time being but in the end rejected for lack of funds. In 1900 the Fort Herrick property was valued at $50 an acre, and its worth was increasing steadily. In addition, the Commander gave a higher priority to the larger colonies in California and Colorado, especially because they were irrigated. Irrigation and intensive cultivation of small holdings of cheap land were the essential ingredients of successful colonization, he came to believe.[27]

Colony families were relocated. Even before the decision, John Vrieling and Augustus Priebe had migrated to Fort Amity; Vrieling was again to move and take up land at Fort Romie. One family was still at Fort Herrick when Haggard visited in 1905; another had been taken into partnership by two sisters who owned a farm nearby; still another bought a small farm in the neighborhood on installments. No settlers, as such, remained.[28] Fort Herrick had been given a new mission.

Located nine miles from the nearest bar, it became a haven for alcoholics, with its apparatus of fields, dairy, poultry sheds, and pigeon cotes all intact to provide both employment and income. But within a few years, the Army sold off much of its farm equipment and part of its land and turned the rest into a "Fresh Air Camp for the Children of Cleveland," a use which continued into the 1970s. When final negotiations were underway for sale of the camp property in 1974, Colonel John Waldron wrote: "This closes out a chapter in Army history since Ft. Herrick is the last remaining property used formerly as a Farm Colony in Booth-Tucker's day."[29]

CHAPTER SEVEN

The Dollars and Cents of Colonization

There is a new salvation scheme.
Three public wastings to redeem:
Our landless, manless capital
To make the waste relieve the want
The Salvation Army, without daunt,
Proposed three Colonies to run.
And this is how 'tis done. [1]

IN SUMMING UP ITS "CALL TO ARMS" for 1897 and part of 1898, the Salvation Army noted that its farm colonies had passed successfully "through the first and most perilous year of their existence." In September 1898 the three settlements totaled 1,400 acres of "rich agricultural land" and boasted 160 colonists and an aggregate value of land and improvements "close upon $100,000." All this, said the editor of the Pacific edition of *The War Cry*, constituted the beginnings of "a gigantic Social revolution, the results and benefits of which are bound to reach millions of hearts and homes."[2] When the Army scheduled its "Grand Anniversary Rally" for Carnegie Hall in mid-December of the same year, it listed its farm colonies among it featured accomplishments. Booth-Tucker addressed the assembly in order to detail "the progress of the great colonization scheme"; those in attendance could view a "Marvelous Stereopticon and Kinetoscope Display" and a "Model Cottage of our Colonies, and a Windmill, through which the poor will pass from Poverty to Plenty." This promotional activity was designed primarily to raise funds, and the Commander could express satisfaction with the proposal of former New York *Tribune* editor John E. Milholland, who suggested a meeting of "some leading City gentlemen" to develop a source of capital.[3]

Early financing of the settlements had been both haphazard and precarious. It had been based on loan or gift money solicited privately through sympathetic self-interest groups like the San Francisco Committee of Fifteen or at the large open public meetings in Carnegie Hall, Chicago, or San Francisco. A few "angels" like Milholland or Mark Hanna were helpful. When the Booth-Tuckers visited Cleveland in a drive to raise $20,000 for Fort Herrick, Hanna donated $1,000, and then in his own hand drew up a list of fifty prominent citizens, many of them in Washington, whom the Consul should approach, using his name. "It was a magic document," according to a New York newspaper. "When these men saw the Senator's handwriting they subscribed at once, and the money was quickly realized." Actually, according to the Salvation Army balance sheet to September 30, 1902, only $13,845 were collected in Cleveland, although more may have been donated elsewhere.[4]

But "angels" were in short supply, and much of the support pledged was in the form of individual loans which ultimately had to be repaid, sometimes at inopportune moments.[5] Still, the Army worked ceaselessly to convince wealthy Americans of the worthiness of the colony investment, using the testimonials of mayors, governors, jurists, cabinet members, or industrialists, among others, to help convince the wary.[6] At the time of the Spanish American War, Booth-Tucker wondered about priorities:

> It is a disgrace to us as a nation that while we stretch forth our eager hands and empty millions out of our treasure vaults, and pour forth our life's blood to rescue the wretched Cubans, we should permit three millions of our fellow citizens to rot and perish at our very doors.[7]

But in the beginning, so long as the colonies remained purely experimental and unproven, money was difficult to raise. "Make one of these a success and thereby demonstrate their feasibility," one of the country's millionaires told Booth-Tucker, "and you will never need to trouble about the funds required for the enterprise."[8]

At various times, in addition to approaching individuals and making mass appeals at fervent meetings, the Army tried other fund-raising approaches, including a "Colony Chain" proposal of 1900, which seems never to have developed satisfactorily. At one point, Booth-Tucker contemplated creation of a central national council, made up of men of influence, patterned after the San Francisco Chamber of Commerce Committee of Fifteen, to cooperate with subcommittees in each state, county or city "where suitable openings may exist," and to invite the support of philanthropists, capitalists, and landowners. The results, he was sure, would ". . . prove to the most Malthusian mind that, after all, God is not mistaken in allowing the existence of so many human beings. . . ."[9] In the end, however, the national council never materialized.

In an effort to create more orderly and on-going financing, Army spokesman in the summer of 1900 announced the chartering in New York of a Salvation Army Colonization Company, with a nominal capital of $300,000, of which 151,000 shares were to be retained by the Army and 149,000 offered for sale, the latter to pay "a guaranteed dividend of 5% per annum paid semi-annually." With further information available from Booth-Tucker at National Headquarters in New York, John Milsaps of the Pacific edition of *The War Cry* urged his readers to subscribe: "Help, then, 'the man behind the plow' to plant, to cultivate and to bring to fruition the Salvation Army Colonization scheme."[10]

But apparently this corporate plan was abandoned without shares being sold in favor of a bond alternative. In its charter of incorporation by the New York legislature in 1899, the Salvation Army gave the following as one of its aims:

> . . . to establish farm colonies in any of the states or territories of the United States for the purpose of enabling the working classes of the great cities of the United States who desire to own their own homes, and other persons who have no homes of their own to acquire homesteads and become self-supporting by tilling the soil. . . .

Along with authorizing the Army to acquire real property, construct buildings, and advance money to colonists, the act of incorporation also gave general powers to carry out colonization objectives and granted the right to borrow money and issue bonds secured by a mortgage on the farm-colony lands if the five Salvation Army trustees agreed unanimously.[11] The Army had deliberately worded this section and had lobbied hard for its passage in order to have maximum flexibility in the raising of funds and also, if possible, to free the colonies from taxation, an end which was never achieved, except for the Cherry Tree Home at Amity.[12]

Early in 1901, under the umbrella of its act of incorporation, in the interest of consolidating the loans already contracted and of providing a more stable financial base, as well as expanding the colonization experiments, the Army announced an issue of $150,000 in thirty-year gold bonds, bearing five percent interest paid semi-annually. These $500 bonds were secured by a mortgage on Fort Romie and Fort Amity, a mortgage held by the North American Trust Company of New York, acting as trustees for the bondholders. A sinking fund of two percent paid yearly to North American was to give further security and the public was assured of an "ABSOLUTELY SAFE investment."[13] There were still a few bonds available as late as February 1903 but subscriptions were soon complete. At the end of September of the following year, fifty-five individuals and two Salvation Army divisions accounted for the entire $150,000. International Headquarters held $15,000 worth; among the private bondholders were Mark Hanna ($1,000); General Benjamin F. Tracy, former Secretary of the Navy ($1,000); J. C. Havemeyer, wealthy sugar refiner ($6,000); Warner Van Norden, president of the Bank of North America ($500); and Charles P. Fagnani, professor at Union Theological Seminary ($9,000). Noticeable, too, was the fact that some of the largest subscribers were women: Fannie A. Whitmore held $16,000 and Ida M. Mason, $40,000.[14]

Along with the bond issue, the Army also sought to encourage small donors and lenders and created the Century Endowment Fund, to which gifts of as little as $10 were solicited. Booth-Tucker hoped that this account would ultimately total $100,000, and that the money would be loaned to colonists and reloaned to others as soon as it was repaid. The Commander estimated that in ten years $100,000 could establish a total of 523 families, of whom 200 would have paid off all debts and would own their farms outright at the end of a decade. To advertise the fund, which in 1903 had reached $30,000, Booth-Tucker circulated an illustrated forty-five-page pamphlet, *Prairie Homes For City Poor*, with an application form on the back cover.[15] Whether this is the same as the Colonization Loan Account carried on the Army's books after 1904 is not clear. That account, totaling $38,297.43 at the end of September 1904 recorded smaller loans from some businesses, for example, the Earle Fruit Company and the State Bank of California ($100 each), but mainly from individuals, among whom were a number of Salvation Army officers, including colorful "Joe the Turk" Garabed

($200) and Thomas Holland ($1,500).[16] The Colonization Loan Account reached its peak in 1904, then tapered off until 1914.

COLONIZATION LOAN ACCOUNT[17]

Year	Amount
1904	38,297.43
1906	37,062.51
1908	32,931.30
1910	17,542.11
1911	13,974.00
1914	11,875.00

After the untimely death of the Consul in October 1903, Commander Booth-Tucker inaugurated a new and separate campaign to raise $50,000. The drive was to be in the hands of Colonel Holland, who had been seriously injured in the same accident that killed the Consul. The account, said Booth-Tucker, "... will be known as the Emma Booth-Tucker Colony Memorial Fund, in memory of my beloved wife, who felt the keenest interest in the welfare of our Colonies, and indeed sacrificed her life on their behalf."[18] How much this fund brought in is uncertain; nor is it clear whether the Santa Fe Railroad's reported contribution of $10,000 in the Consul's name to reopen the Cherry Tree Home as a tuberculosis sanitarium was a part of it or whether it was separate.[19]

Salvation Army records also refer to other sources of money. In 1904, for example, the books showed $2,500 transferred from the Harvest Festival to the colony accounts. In 1905, they showed $2,000 in Self-Denial funds, money which came traditionally from soldiers and officers of the Army who made personal sacrifices to raise it. At the same time, another $10,088.28 was shown as coming from "Colony Appeals," probably an ongoing campaign, although any new emergency might trigger special efforts. For example, the saline problem and the attendant tiling expense at Amity would prompt specific appeals and mailings to provide stopgap financing. Among colony income sources reflected in the 1907 balance sheets were donations—$1,700.76; "Appropriation from Self-Denial Fund"—$5,000; and "Appropriation from Harvest Festival Fund"—$15,000.[20]

Loans had their disadvantages. Private loans were sometimes tied to a particular piece of land or area; many were short term and too often they came due or were called in at embarrassing times. And above all, they were expensive. Interest payments had to be met, even though colonists failed to meet their obligations. The Central Colonization

Department paid out $15,222.32 in interest on loans and bonds for fiscal 1904 and $14,885.22 for fiscal 1907.[21]

In addition to the expense involved, the quirks of the New York laws governing incorporation of the Salvation Army and the liquidation of mortgage indebtedness invoked awkward and time-consuming procedures before land title might pass to individual colonists or indeed to any other purchaser. By the 1899 act of incorporation, the Army might sell or mortgage its real property only after meeting the provisions of the code of civil procedure, which required the permission of the New York Supreme Court for each transaction. At the same time, any transfer of even a few acres (or even a townsite lot) meant that that proportion of the mortgage bonds be retired with the North American Trust Company or its successors. Thus each time a colonist had met his full obligation or an outsider wished to make a purchase, the Army could not provide a valid deed, no matter how small the land parcel, until it had obtained legal approval from the New York court and had officially paid off a corresponding portion of its mortgage debt with the trust company.[22]

Such burdensome procedures kept the Army's legal counsel hopping in New York. At one point, he complained that Fort Amity alone "monopolizes about one-third of the time that I have to give to my office work." When some of the lots on the Fort Romie townsite were sold to noncolonists, attorney Madison Ferris sought to retire the entire townsite from the mortgage so as not to be troubled with each individual lot, but the process went on for a year-and-a-half without action. For his part, manager Nels Erikson advised that the townsite not be mentioned by name, lest the trust company require a higher proportionate price than for farmland before releasing title.[23] Further complication and delay was to come in 1905 and again in 1912, when the North American Trust Company merged with other firms and became first the Trust Company of America and subsequently the Equitable Trust Company.[24]

Invariably there were legal gaffes that might postpone final release of titles. At Romie a number of title deeds were duly cleared in New York and put on record in Salinas without the required notarized signatures of the recipients. In 1903, Thomas Holland discovered that small amount chattel mortgages which were an integral part of land and livestock contracts had a life of no longer than two years in Colorado unless specifically renewed. At Romie, as late as 1907, the deed to the colony was still in Booth-Tucker's name and had to be changed legally.[25]

The floating of the mortgage bond issue of 1901 created some concerns in the minds of colonists both at Romie and Amity. Holland reported from Colorado in November of that year that settlers exhibited "a high state of feeling" and "a very considerable amount of anxiety everywhere as to our ability to deliver title." It was commonly (and falsely) assumed, even by officers of the Amity Land Company, that the bond issue had tied up all land title for thirty years. For his part, Holland pledged an all-out effort to counteract this attitude and to "put an effectual quietus on the affair forever" by delivering title to the first colonist who met his obligation, Charles Stimson of Fort Amity.[26]

A native of Illinois, Stimson had lived in Canada and in western Kansas before moving to Colorado. With money from the sale of his Kansas farm, he was one of the few colonists with capital and had put down $600 on his land. By the autumn of 1901, he had completed his financial responsibilities to the Army and actively sought the deed to his property. What he discovered first of all was that the deed to all Fort Amity lands had been filed in the name of Commander Booth-Tucker, not the Salvation Army, a revelation that caused considerable consternation at the colony.[27] Although Ferris in New York thought Simpson's fears "the height of impudence," he saw no problem. Booth-Tucker should simply make the deed over to the Army. Meanwhile, the land absolutely was not frozen until 1931: the bond arrangement permitted a piecemeal liquidation of debt. But, Ferris confided to Holland, the Army had no obligation to explain to the colonists until they fulfilled their legal obligations.[28]

Stimson's title was slow to clear, although Holland considered it an important test case. "Something will really have to be done for this man or we shall certainly have troubles," he predicted. "As it is, there is a general impression circulating all around that we cannot give title." Ferris responded that he was at work drawing up the deed, but that Stimson still owed $488.73. To clear the title, he would have to pay the North American Trust Company, "and just at present, there is no need of my telling you, we are a little short." There were further complications: with the property still in Booth-Tucker's name, Ferris discovered that because they were coequal commanders in the United States, both Emma and Frederick must sign the documents.[29] Apparently Holland was slow in forwarding Stimson's checks to National Headquarters, which caused additional delay, as did the discovery that the North American Trust Company had improperly filed its mortgage at the Prowers County courthouse in 1901. When Ferris discovered that the anti-alcohol clause had not been incorporated in the deed, there was another postponement.[30]

Late in July 1902 the property transfer still had not been completed, and Stimson and Holland were now embroiled in a dispute over interest charges. "He does not want to pay any interest at all from the time he took possession," Holland reported. Ferris was not surprised but was wary of adverse public opinion. ". . . We cannot afford to fight with any of our colonists, even if they refuse to pay for the land at all." The best solution, he suggested, was to give Stimson his deed and settle the interest question later. The cash Stimson had paid in was needed to help pay the trust company to release the title of Fort Romie land to Oscar Lindstrand, who by then was also "howling for his deed."[31]

When Booth-Tucker visited Amity in the summer, he reached an accord with Stimson, agreeing that clauses relating to irrigation and maintenance of shade trees should be deleted. The decision required Ferris to draw up a new instrument, which he had done by September. But then Stimson, to no avail, questioned the no-liquor provision and the fact that Booth-Tucker had signed with initials only, although his full name appeared in the body of the document. "If all the colonists hang us up in the same way," Ferris complained, "I'm afraid the results of this scheme . . . will be even worse than my prognostications."[32]

It was late in January of 1903 when Ferris forwarded the revised deed, which he assumed would "now suit His Royal Highness." Apparently it did not. Two months later the lawyer once again sent the rewritten deed to Stimson's wife, Ada, hoping that it was satisfactory.[33] This time it was. Records indicate that while the North American Trust Company had released Stimson's land in May 1902 legal title did not pass from the Army until the end of March, nearly a year later.[34] It was unfortunate that the first settler to seek legal possession at Amity was involved in such a complex and frustrating experience. If nothing else, at the end of nearly three years of negotiation, he received his land and in the process proved that, mortgage debt or none, title was not tied up.

In 1906, when Fort Amity was in travail, Nels Erikson, who had just been reassigned from Romie as manager, stressed the importance of the colonies to the Salvation Army. The colonization plan, he thought, was somehow "divinely inspired, and the launching of it was God's way of bringing the Army out of the difficulties which beset it after the split, by turning the thoughts of our people from our sorrow to the important work we had in hand." Once created, the Army was duty-bound to protect its settlement program, for it had become a highly publicized and integral part of the Army and any withdrawal would weaken the whole. Colonization had brought prestige and public stature. Any acknowledgment that the scheme was a failure would be a severe blow to the Salvation Army.

To prevent such a disaster, Erikson suggested changes in basic colony financing to throw the burden upon the provincial centers, rather than upon National Headquarters. The Army should sell its interest in Fort Amity to a corporation to be organized like several other Army components—the Reliance Trading Company or the Industrial Homes Company. This new Amity Improvement Company would be capitalized at $100,000, fifty-one percent of which would be held by the Army, with the balance to be sold to improve the property. It would assume payment of principal and interest on two-thirds of the existing bond issue—$100,000.

The Army would also dispose of its Fort Romie holding to a new Fort Romie Improvement Company, to be capitalized at $25,000, of which $13,000 in stock would remain in Army hands and the remainder sold for acquiring land under option and for general improvements. For its part, the Fort Amity Improvement Company would assume payment of principal and interest of one-third of the bond issue, or $50,000.

Such a readjustment, Erikson believed, would show a serious loss on the colonies, "but it is better to show this loss now than to show a greater one later." The Army could never hope to pay the full amount of interest, he said, much less contributions to the sinking funds. Moreover, the amount charged against the individual colonies was far beyond their real value; "in fact the values can only be considered theoretical or book values, and are getting further and further away from the real intrinsic worth of the properties." To realize $150,000 for the Amity colony and $75,000 for Romie "would be doing very well," even though such a readjustment would suggest that the Salvation Army was perhaps $100,000 poorer. What should govern was the real market value, not inflated book figures. Erikson thought there was nothing discreditable about the physical conditions encountered by the Army at Amity. Depreciating drainage expenses or the costs of launching the scheme did not warrant criticism, he believed, but creating a false impression by inflating colony property values certainly did.

Erikson believed it would be wise for the Army to make an annual grant of $5,000 to Amity and $2,000 to Romie for management expenses and let the colonies "dig out their own carrying charges." Romie could do so immediately; Amity could do so only when its lands were reclaimed and returned to productivity, which might take several years.[35]

Despite Erikson's fears, the Army was able to meet its long-term obligations early: in 1917 all of the thirty-year bonds were retired and mortgage release was given by the Equitable Trust Company of New York, which a few years earlier had merged with the North American Trust Company. No doubt, as the Army's auditors had predicted, the reinvestment of the mandatory sinking fund was a positive factor in paying off the debt ahead of time.[36] The separate mortgage on the Amity land, first held by the Amity Land Company and then by the

Arkansas Valley Sugar Beet and Irrigated Land Company, was gradually trimmed from $27,740 in 1902 until by 1914 it had been liquidated.[37]

Precisely how much the Salvation Army had invested in the colony experiment is difficult to say. Early in 1902, Booth-Tucker reported publicly that to date a total of $184,833 had gone into the three settlements, while at the same time colonists had made payments of $12,539.60. According to the Commander, these expenditures fell into several categories: $21,806 for management costs; $57,115 for improvements, including irrigation; $48,846 in advances to settlers; $16,450 for interest; and $40,616 for land.[38] Yet Army records indicate that land purchases for Amity and Romie alone by the time of Booth-Tucker's statement totaled $73,400.65, more than eighty percent above the Commander's figures for all three colonies.[39] To further compound the financial picture, the Army carried its real estate on its books "at the reduced price for which the land is sold to the colonists"—$81,170.35 in the case of Fort Amity; $53,000.00 for Fort Romie; and $14,400.00 for Fort Herrick.[40] Invariably, when discussing losses or lauding the successes of its colonies, officers spoke of "the enhanced market value of the land." Thus, according to the 1902 balance sheet published by the Central Colonization Department, the land at Amity was calculated to be worth at least $200,000; that at Romie, $75,000; and Herrick, $20,000.[41]

This was a tenuous business, of course, and leaders such as Nels Erikson could well be concerned about carrying property on the books at inflated prices. Eventually, much of this would simply have to be written off. Total colony property and equipment in 1907 were valued on the balance sheet at $189,936.29, of which land and improvements constituted $118,673.41.[42] Three years later, these figures had been cut nearly in half on the books, although only one colonist had received title to his property in that period.[43] Totals continued to dwindle until 1920, when liabilities of $23,473.83 and assets of $11,648.10, all in contracts, were written off and the colony account closed.[44]

In any event, although financial sheets often obscure as much as they reveal, the colonies represented a substantial investment on the part of the Salvation Army. The Central Colonization Department's printed figures in 1905 showed bond and loan liabilities of $185,999.68, not to mention the Amity land mortgage, then at $19,937.98, plus an internal loan total which had just been reduced to $37,306.23 by special grants to the colonies earlier in the year. Everything included, on the books at least, the Army had more than $330,000 involved.[45]

Unfortunately, there is no way of telling exactly how much of this was inflated or how much of a return there was from colonists in meeting their obligations. Individual colonists' accounts are incomplete, but the message they convey from Amity especially is that a substantial amount of debt was never repaid. Haggard estimated that the Army lost some $27,000 on the first group of drought-ridden colonists at Romie. Other writers believe that Amity brought losses of from $60,000 to $70,000,[46] probably a conservative estimate. But stalwart supporters argued that even so, despite drought, high interest rates, and misjudgment of beginning production costs, the colonies "as a whole" proved the feasibility of placing city men, ignorant of agriculture, onto the land, provided they were directed by those with sufficient farm knowledge. Had General Booth been able to carry out a large-scale colonization project, the results, based on the limited California and Colorado experience, would have furnished "a permanent memorial to his interest in the land problem." Even so, the human side of land settlement was more important than the economic and more difficult to judge. In the end, it was argued, the "Heavenly auditors" would assess the books on that score.[47]

While National Colonization Secretary Holland and Commander and Consul Booth-Tucker were important figures in the collection of funds, they also played major roles in the allocation of those monies, at least until the Consul's death in the autumn of 1903. Soon after the colonies were organized—by June 1898, at least—Booth-Tucker had created a Colonization Council, over which he presided, and whose members included other high Army officials: Richard Holz, Madison Ferris, Major Gustav S. Reinhardsen, Brigadiers Cox and Caygill, Edward Higgins, and occasionally Thomas Holland.[48]

Meeting weekly in New York City, the Colonization Council or Colonization Board, as it was sometimes called, exercised control over individual colony finances. It scrutinized invoices sent from the colonies and approved or disapproved specific items. It instructed Holland to systematize matters by entering all purchases in a special ledger before asking New York for payment. It decided as a matter of policy that Army capital would not ordinarily be used to establish colony stores, although negotiations with and subsidies of private parties were encouraged, and the Army subsequently did own a share or two in the Fort Romie cooperative store.[49] Perhaps because Thomas Holland was less involved with it than with the other settlements, Fort Herrick seems to have borne the brunt of the Council's early cheese-paring policies. Or perhaps manager Bourne's requests were not as carefully thought out as those from Romie or Amity. Whatever the reason, Bourne must have felt penned in by the negative reactions to his various proposals and by constant reminders to exercise frugality.[50]

In 1899, the Colonization Council was either replaced by or merged with the more general Finance Council, which was also to be

made up of at least six members, of whom three were ex officio
President, First Vice President, and Second Vice President of the
Salvation Army Board of Trustees. The Council was now charged with
overseeing expenditures not only for the farm colonies, but for training homes, lodging shelters, rescue and rest homes, and the National
Headquarters.[51] In either body, as chairman and by virtue of his
position in the Salvation Army, Commander Booth-Tucker wielded
tremendous influence.

Like its predecessor, the Finance Council sought to channel all
income from the colonies through the official books in New York and to
handle directly all bills due creditors in the west. These awkward and
cumbersome procedures soon broke down and seem to have been
more honored in the breach than in practice. In time, the National
Headquarters provided each colony with a weekly stipend on a regular
basis, with most expenditures approved as a matter of routine by the
Council, except for unusual outlays, as, for example, the heavy costs of
tiling and drainage at Amity in 1906–1907.[52]

Although undertaken "in a spirit of philanthropy," with the Army
contributing managerial costs—estimated to be as much as $2,500 a
year in California or more than $4,900 over-all—officials always spoke
of the colonies as business propositions and accordingly kept intricate
and detailed accounts of all expenditures, on a daily basis, of colonists'
accounts, or by such categories as real estate, loans, furnishings, or
administrative costs.[53] Records extant for both Romie and Amity for
the 1900–1910 period indicate that cash flow was largely one-way in an
east to west direction. Army expenditures greatly outweighed income
produced by the settlers. For the first half-dozen years, income at Fort
Romie included the regular forty-dollar weekly contribution from
National Headquarters, plus small payments on rent, interest, or returns on pigs or poultry. From the beginning, Fort Amity colonists
were heavily dependent upon New York. For the period from April 8,
1900, to September 27, 1901, inclusive, during part of which the
Cherry Tree Home was under construction, the Colorado colony had a
cash income of $39,114.40, of which $35,206.85 or more than ninety
percent came from National Headquarters. Apart from that, cash flow
came mainly from post office receipts, settlers' individual payments
(rarely large), home farm crops, or pasturage rental.[54]

On the other hand, until income stepped up considerably as it did
at Romie about 1908 (but not at Amity), colony expenditures, either in
loans or direct payments, went primarily for building materials, home
farm equipment, fencing, livestock, and wages. Especially in the first
half-dozen years, heavy outlays went into labor costs to colonists, whose
land, livestock, or other accounts were credited with work of all kinds,

especially plowing, blacksmithing, hauling crops, or moving buildings. At Amity, the construction of the two schoolhouses, the Cherry Tree Home, and individual farms or officers' homes provided much needed wages, especially in the winter months.[55] At both western colonies, a good deal of money went into development and support of the irrigation systems. At Amity, building laterals and, after 1906, draining and tiling required a heavy investment of labor and capital. At Romie, between 1900 and 1903, much went into support of the irrigation system—directly for lumber, canvas, or even rubber boots, or more indirectly in the form of $1,100.00 for fuel for the wood-burning steam plant in 1900; $175.00 for labor in 1901 "cutting Ditch from Pumping Plant to the Salinas River"; $650.00 for pump repairs in 1902; or $155.00 for a car of coal oil for the new Fort Romie Water Company a year later; or even $56.50 to enable the water company to meet its tax bill.[56]

Administrative salaries were not large, but individual Army Officers, even colonists such as John Vrieling at Romie and Joseph Hargreaves and William J. Carter at Amity received a "weekly grant"; in Vrielings's case it was six dollars, for the others five dollars. Ensign French asked for three dollars in Colorado, but received only two dollars. After Staff Captain James Burrows was "Promoted to Glory" in March 1906, the Army continued to supply money for clothing, shoes, and supplies for the Burrows children at Amity. Nels Erikson received $12 a week as manager at Romie and Colonel Holland, whether as supervisor at Amity or as National Colonization Secretary, drew regularly upon National Headquarters for both salary and travel.[57]

Records indicate numerous subsidies, both for the colonies in general and for individual settlers. Even after the original settlers, the Army paid travel expenses of colonists, where necessary. It provided loan support for settlement—"cows and cottages," as it were. In a number of instances at Amity the Army paid out $300.00 each for houses for new families and in 1902 authorized three more at $500.00 each. Locating the Smith family in 1903, and providing house, fencing, team, and implements, cost the Army $487.15; settling the Craftons and the Grindrods in 1904 took $500.00 apiece. At Fort Romie, the Army contributed $50.00 for the new home of A. C. Carle; $100.00 "for Building to be erected for Colonist Bushnell"; and $320.00 for "locating C. F. Jernquist as a colonist."[58]

Other expenditures might include "cows for colonists," medicine for sick livestock or even "feed for bull." At both Amity and Romie, the Army provided funds for prizes at the annual "Gala Days" competition to award excellence in farming; at Romie, it also gave prizes to school children. At both colonies, it set aside funds for Christmas turkeys and other holiday expenses. It paid the twenty-five dollar audit fee charged by Staff Captain Hamon, the national auditor, besides laying out thirteen dollars for entertainment of Hamon and Holland who visited Romie at the same time. It contributed $100 for a Kinetoscope for the Amity Institute and took care of entertaining the organizer of the Farmers' Institute and a special post office agent at Fort Romie; and it even picked up three dollars for "loss on horse trade" at the Colorado settlement.[59]

Despite Booth-Tucker's invariable optimism and the roseate statements of the press, the colonists were slow to meet their obligations. Returns to national headquarters from proceeds of crops and livestock were rarely forthcoming, and delinquencies irritated Madison Ferris in New York. "When, for gracious sake, are we going to get the money from this years harvest from them, or are they going to try to bilk us out of that?" he asked Thomas Holland in 1901.[60] A year later he was looking forward "to at least $10,000 hard cold cash" from Amity "from long deferred payments,"[61] money that never materialized. And in 1904 he signed his usual lament of colony hard times with sarcasm to the manager:

> Trusting that you and your good wife are enjoying the best of health and becoming rich and prosperous with the great overflow of cash pouring in from the colonies—which you always seem, however, to keep in your midst—I am. . . .[62]

Ferris seemed perpetually frustrated. He complained that the financial council spent most of its time approving expenditures for the colonies; that the Army was much too generous and relaxed where the settlers were concerned; and that national headquarters rarely knew what was going on at Amity and Romie. "It's the hardest work in the world for anybody to find out head or tail of any of these colonies," he said. "I've been trying for four years to find out; and I know less about them today than I did when I started."[63] Amity ". . . really needs one man to attend to nothing but its wants," he told Holland. "As the drafts for that Colony pour in upon us, and no money ever coming to us from it, I tell you plainly I don't see the way out." He did suggest creation of a colony department in New York to handle details that were lost among the other matters handled by the board of trustees and the financial council: ". . . otherwise, money will run away from us and we won't know where it has gone to."[64]

No such department was formed; nor were Booth-Tucker, Holland and other enthusiasts openly concerned about the colonists' collective debt. They explained that poor people without capital must of necessity spend what their farms produced in order to live and to buy livestock and implements and make improvements "so as to warrant the prospect of their being able to do much better as a result." Holland noted in 1905 that the Army had not foreclosed on any settler, but inasmuch as the colonies were not charity but business propositions, colonists would eventually have to meet their obligations in order to gain title to their lands.[65] If they defaulted, which was too often the case, it was the Army's loss. Nonpayers simply left or sold to third parties, perhaps gaining little or nothing for their investment of time and labor, and leaving the Army to begin anew with another family. In this respect, Ferris was right: the Salvation Army was a soft-hearted creditor, unwilling, or perhaps unable, to exert real pressure on those who lagged.

CHAPTER EIGHT

The Colony Balance Sheet

> *We all know that the Army, as a whole, has benefitted very largely through the Colonization Scheme. It has given us prestige, and placed us in an enviable position before the public. If we were forced to admit that the colonies were a failure, the confidence that the best men in the country have in us would be shaken, and it would be a blow from which we could hardly recover.*[1]

IF SUCCESS IS TO BE MEASURED by how many colonists became independent landowners as result of the Salvation Army experiment, what then can be said about Amity, Romie, and Herrick? What of colonist mobility, persistence in meeting payments to the Army, and the ultimate disposition of the land involved? Because Fort Herrick was early abandoned as a farm colony and the fate of most of its eight or ten families obscured, it falls in a separate category. Clearly, Fort Romie was the most successful of the three in that a higher percentage of its settlers obtained deeds to their property; after the initial years, Romie had no serious dislocations comparable to the alkali crisis that beset the Colorado colony a half dozen years after its founding.

Both colonies experienced periods of instability. By 1901, all but one of the original Romie settlers had departed, victims of prolonged drought. At Amity, according to the always optimistic Booth-Tucker in

1902, only three colonists had withdrawn: one who was dissatisfied, one who was killed in a railroad accident, and one who left because of a seriously ill wife.[2] When Haggard asked about settler mobility in Colorado in 1905, he was told that from sixteen to eighteen families had left Amity, each for his or her own reason, but never because the land failed to provide a living. Several went because of ill health, their own or that of a family member; some believed they could do better as farmers elsewhere; several with mechanical or trade skills took land near larger towns, to combine farming and their crafts; and, according to Holland, the opening of free land in the Canadian Northwest lured away "several of our families" who were of Canadian background.[3]

Some ignored their farming to follow other pursuits. Holland described E. D. Cox as "one of our pioneer colonists," who "has not made a success of farming." By then, Cox had long been in default of payments and no longer lived on his land, but worked for the Holly sugar beet company.[4] German-born Robart Rupp who arrived in 1899, sold out at a profit of $626.00 in the fall of 1902 to take "an important position at 72½ [¢] an hour in Chicago."[5] Original settler James H. Childs in 1902 sold his Amity farmland to concentrate on his store; seven years later, George Thomas—farmer, grocer, and for a time county sheriff—solved part of his $2682.50 debt problem by turning his agricultural land back to the Army, but keeping his mercantile property.[6]

If a colonist stayed only briefly, as in the case of Sam Dean of Syracuse, Kansas, who in 1900 took up an allotment at Amity but within a few weeks had packed up and moved out,[7] there was no settlement taking into account improvements. But most colonists lasted several years, at least, and their debts to the Army and their improvements to land and buildings both increased. Thus when a family left Amity or Romie, financial adjustments were necessary. As Colonel Holland told Charles Barkman, who had moved away to the state of Washington, the Army would prefer him to return and carry out his contract, on which he owed $1,914.41, but it had not objected to his selling the land, provided he paid off his debt.[8] On occasions, it simply cancelled the contract if there were extenuating circumstances. For example, in 1905, when J. Carr asked to give up his Amity land, the Army was quite willing to nullify the agreement. "I may say he is an old man and a bachelor, and past the age where he is able to do any work himself...," manager James Durand explained.[9]

Fort Romie records do not indicate the nature of Army settlements with colonists who sold their rights to others before meeting their obligations. They do show that C. H. Hume had been at Romie five years and owed $3,048.60 when his holding was taken over by the

Nelson Brothers, John and Frank, near the end of September 1908.
The Nelsons had another account of their own with the Salvation Army
which they managed to cut in half between 1903 and 1913, for land,
some of which they acquired title to eventually.[10] Charles Handley, a
seven-year veteran, owed the Army $2,800.87 by the end of September
1910, then turned the property over to William A. Rothe, who four
years later paid it off.[11] Arioslo Carle had been at Romie nine years
before he transferred his account—on which he owed $1,500—to
Fred Evans, who paid it off within eighteen months.[12] Salvationist John
Vrieling, who was in debt $2,097.74 in 1912, sold his allotment to the
Ladies Aid Society in Romie in 1915, but there is no indication of the
distribution of proceeds between him and the Army.[13]

Fort Amity accounts are often more specific and make it clear that
most colonists who left before their full time were so deeply in debt to
the Army that they received relatively small adjustments when their
accounts were settled. After nearly ten years, George H. Thomas,
$2,682.50 in debt, turned his farm property back to the Army in 1909
and received $320.00 in the settlement.[14] In the same year, after nine
years, George Nicol transferred his holdings to a third party, and the
Army settled with him for $429.32.[15] George Waidner, who came from
Baltimore in 1901, admitted four years later that he had paid the Army
"a little of my indebtedness, but not as much as I should." Late in 1905,
he paid for his cow, but returned land, buildings, and equipment to
the Army, which paid him $231.75.[16] In other instances, the Army
settled with colonists who left after two years, paying them $167.00 and
$109.17 respectively.[17] On the other hand, it settled with Frank
McAbee, owner of the quarry and in debt for $1,792.26 in 1908, for a
total of $1,125.22.[18]

At Amity, particularly, contracts were likely to change hands several times. For example, that originally held by Alfred Cash was passed
on to W. H. Hammock in 1902, then assigned to W. H. Manning in
1903, when the first payment of any kind was made to the Army.
Subsequently, Manning transferred the contract to M. J. Wiley of
Emporia, Kansas, who sold the property in 1912 to J. A. Ziegler. Ziegler
had taken an allotment of his own in 1902, but five years later relinquished it to the Army, still owing more than $522 on it.[19] When
store owner James Childs in 1902 transferred his farm allotment to
J. S. McMurtry to devote more attention to his business, the land
was then purchased by William S. Greenard, who acquired it as a "good
safe investment" in 1904. After Greenard's death, his heirs willed the
property back to the Salvation Army, who again disposed of it to
McMurtry.[20]

Records indicate that of the Romie colonists after 1901, at least seven sold their holdings to third parties before gaining title. Of the Amity group, prior to 1905, eight either returned their allotments to the Army or sold them to others. After 1905, when the saline curse was upon the land, twelve more fell into this category.[21]

In a number of instances colonists died before they had met their full obligations. In such cases, invariably the widows were permitted to remain to keep their families together. At Fort Romie, for example, after her husband, Charles, died in 1904, Anna Johnson continued on the land with her three small children. Her husband had owned a place in the hills, which she sold; she also rented out 9 of her 12.22 Romie acres for $112.00 a year, which more than covered her payments, and on the remaining tract made a profit from cattle and chickens until 1912, when she sold the entire property for $1,590.18, a sum which covered her remaining obligations with some to spare. Also at Romie, C. M. Hodges died in 1906 and his wife, Amy, took over the balance of his debt to the Army—$2,905. Five years later, she remarried and paid $1,000 to gain clear title to at least part of the land; then, in 1913 she sold out for cash.[22] Records indicate that three other Romie wives—the spouses of Samuel Handley, Emil Baetschen, and R. A. Hidalgo—all took over upon the death of their respective husbands and eventually obtained title to the land.[23] At Amity, widow Elisabeth Slaymaker and her three children remained briefly in 1900, and the widow of William Carter, storekeeper and Salvation Army officer, would settle up his business interests, receiving $483.95 in the arrangement from the Army.[24]

Not all colonists were model settlers, and some left under a cloud. When the Amity contract of Alfred Cash was transferred to another settler early in 1902, Colonel Holland explained what happened: "Cash proved to be a very shiftless fellow and one who would not do justice to us."[25] Later in the same year, when B. L. Yourdan contemplated giving up his allotment, he proposed keeping his horses and making a token monthly payment, a suggestion Holland rejected, with the warning that the team would be reposssessed if Yourdan gave up the land. Yourdan ignored the advice, left the colony with the team and other goods "not paid for," was apprehended west of Granada, and "asked by the courts to explain." Subsequently, he relinquished the property belonging to the Army, apparently without litigation or charges brought.[26] There were rumors in 1904 that blacksmith E. M. Cram had absconded with mortgaged goods, including the doors of his cottage.[27] When Holland, with support of the Army Finance Council in 1905 cancelled the contract of E. D. Cox because Cox no longer lived on the land and had long since ceased paying on it, Cox vowed emphatically that he would "neither make payments nor give up the place," although apparently he did the latter.[28]

To a few of the Salvation Army hierarchy such as the dour legal counsel, Madison J. H. Ferris, such episodes were typical: too many colonists were taking advantage of the largesse of the Army and were proving unwilling to fend for themselves. Ferris was careful not to publicize his views, but privately he raved against the lax, easy treatment of the Amity settlers who "ought to be made to earn their living instead of receiving bountiful help at the hands of their organization. . . ." They were, he said, "a lot of ingrates who have been receiving emoluments so generously from our large and open-hearted Commander. . . . If I had my way, I would dispossess the whole gang. They are a disgrace to any community. They've got a soft snap, and are smart enough to know it." Colonists were not honoring their contracts, and it was time to "put up or shut up." If Booth-Tucker were only to send him to Colorado, Ferris promised he would call them together, define their legal rights, read out to each one his deficiencies, and give them one week to pay before beginning ouster proceedings. "Our spiritual work is hampered right and left through the drains that have been made for these soft snappers," he grumbled.[29]

In one sense, Ferris was right. A majority of Amity settlers, at least, made little effort to reduce their debts to the Army. A number, if they paid at all, paid only interest. Nine years after his arrival, Erik Erikson, for example, had obligations of $5,133.61 and had paid nothing beyond interest on his land and building accounts; after a decade, George Thomas had paid nothing on the $1,088.00 he owed for land, $600.00 for buildings and $185.55 for livestock.[30] But a minority at Amity and a larger percentage at Romie gradually whittled away at their debts and eventually paid them off. Both Ferris and Holland early agreed that a firmer policy was required to root settlers more firmly to the soil and to prevent their speculation concerning their places. Stated policy was to allow them no equity in their holdings, except improvements, unless they remained for the full contract term. If they left prior to that time, they were to receive improvement value and whatever principal they had paid over and above taxes, water, six percent interest, and other charges.[31]

A higher percentage of post-1901 colonists at Fort Romie ultimately paid off their obligations and gained title to a part, if not all, of the land alloted than Fort Amity settlers. Noticeable in both cases was the fact that the first to acquire deeds to their land were people with extra funds at their disposal. The first was Oscar Lindstrand, the only remaining original settler at Romie, who in 1902 had met the requirements—probably with inherited money—and was anxious to acquire title to "his ten acre patch," as Holland called it. After nearly eight months of negotiations the deed and release of mortgage cleared, and both Lindstrand and Holland were pleased at this practical demonstration of the Army's ability to deliver title. In 1913, Lindstrand completed title to an additional ten acres and in 1915 to a similar amount.[32]

Lindstrand and the Dane, Mathias Mathiesen, were the two Romie colonists listed in 1905 as owning land outright. But Mathiesen was not a typical settler: he had purchased the Army's home farm of 30.39 acres for cash in 1903 and held a special relationship to the colony.[33] It was not until 1910 that another Fort Romie colonist acquired title to the allotted land. Over the next decade, however, a slow but steady procession began. Included were: Thomas Day (20 acres) and Lucy, wife of R. A. Hidalgo (20 acres), both in 1910; Allen Roddick (21 acres), Ede Harding (5.8 acres) and Amy Hodges Porter (20.62 acres), all in 1911; John Anderson (20 acres) and Winfield J. Scott (19.91 acres), 1914; Catherine Baetschen (20.14 acres), 1916; and David Wheeler Wiley (20 acres), 1917.[34]

This list alone is proof that the Fort Romie settlers after 1900 were stayers and that a good percentage—a majority—gained title to their land. But because of the way title transfers were officially entered at the county level, often with a nominal price or no price at all, and because of the incompleteness of existing Salvation Army records, it is not always possible to determine whether a colonist met his full obligation or whether concessions were made in some instances. In addition to these front-line colonists, third parties who acquired the holdings and rights of settlers may or may not have been treated as colonists by the Army; certainly a number were, and once having taken over accounts several of these once-removed colonists, but hardly urban poor, acquired eventual title. At least half a dozen did so.[35] Moreover at least twenty other different persons received deeds for Fort Romie property from the Salvation Army between 1911 and 1923, with the amount of land involved varying from a town lot to slightly over twenty acres. Some of these were no doubt reversions from colonists; some were of unassigned lands; some may have been boundary adjustments, for so many errors had appeared in the old Haskell survey of 1897 that in 1903 Manager Erikson had a new one made and recorded.[36]

At Fort Amity, the record of colonists "proving up"—of sticking to their allotment, regularly meeting their obligations, and eventually receiving title—was much less impressive. To be sure, a major factor was timing. Fort Romie's difficult times had come at the beginning of the experiment. Fresh settlers and improved irrigation brought regeneration. But Amity's days of woe—the saline poisoning—came late, and the antidote seemed not to be working; thus a restocking with new blood was not feasible. The United States Census of 1910 listed only three of the original settlers still at Amity: James H. Childs, Erik Erikson, and Robert Frewing. A. J. Davy, who had helped build the Amity irrigation system and later became a colonist, was still in town, as were several other early settlers including Charles Stimson, Louis Kephart, Henry W. Manning, Robert Newman, Carl Erikson, and Joseph Hargreaves. But only Erik Erikson, Stimson, Manning, and Hargreaves were listed as farmers; Childs, Newman, and Carl Erikson were all general store merchants; Kephart a rancher; Davy a banker; and Frewing, a plasterer and doer of odd jobs. And only one, Stimson, owned a farm free of mortgage; only one, Childs, owned his own home outright.

Stimson had brought the first test case to gain title to his property and had succeeded in 1903, but nobody else followed the same course until 1915, when Carl Erikson paid off the last $666 on ten acres and received his deed. In 1920, in exchange for a final payment of $400, he received an additional ten acres.[37] John Davy acquired twenty acres in 1907, paying $1,170, then sold them to Joseph McMurtry for $2,500 a few years later.[38] Robert P. Frewing had acquired 4.79 acres in 1911 for $95, although his account a year earlier showed that he owed the Army well over $2,800 total.[39] Another colonist, Lewis H. Kephart, who had introduced commercial sheep-raising, had expanded his holdings considerably, but had gone bankrupt in 1916. Owing the Army $5,706.51 in 1917, he renegotiated his contract, let part of his land revert, and with a substantial cash payment, covered most of his obligation.[40] Two others, both Salvation Army officers, were also involved, even after the colony was, in effect, broken up. Joseph H. Hargreaves remained in charge of the buildings for nineteen years, even after the Cherry Tree Home had been razed, and he farmed on a small scale. By 1920, Hargreaves owed the Army $5,642.21, with little hope of liquidation. It was probably in recognition of loyalty and long service that the Army in 1922 deeded Hargreaves an unspecified amount of land at Amity.[41] Tradition also has it that another former officer, "Amity" Frank McGrath, stayed on until World War II, living on an acreage he had been granted and operating a small store,[42] but his name does not appear in the earlier records.

Thus only a handful of Fort Amity colonists achieved the goals of the colonization scheme and attained the status of small independent landholders on their original allotments. But a number remained in the Lamar-Holly area as useful and self-sustaining citizens, often with some property. After it became apparent that the saline crisis was more than a momentary setback, colonists scattered and the Army had no alternative but to get rid of its land as best it could. It sold outright to whomever would buy or granted leases with options to purchase. Transactions were completed with at least sixteen outside buyers between 1909 and 1926.

At both Amity and Romie, part of the land went for uses other than farming. Some of the land in Colorado went in the form of right-of-way to the Holly & Swink Railway Company; 5.11 acres went in an eighty-foot swath to the Santa Fe Railroad in order for the railroad to build a dike to protect both its property and that of the colony from a repetition of the Arkansas River flooding that had done so much damage during the previous year. Additional acres went to the local school district.[43]

At Fort Romie, in 1906, after a hard fight, the Army granted seven lots to the Mission School District as a site for a new building, but school trustees, disagreeing on the location, deeded the property back without breaking ground.[44] Three town lots were granted to the Fort Romie Grange, with the usual anti-liquor stipulation and a caution that the land "shall not be used as a dancing hall."[45] Additional grants went to the Fort Romie Water Company and a small piece of unassigned land was transferred for the erection of a Methodist church.[46] After early 1922 all of the property rights still in Army hands in Colorado and California were transferred to the newly created Salvation Army (of California), but piecemeal distribution of land occasionally continued.[47]

One vestige lingered on: the so-called "morality clause." Except for one transaction in 1919 with the Fort Romie Water Company, all deeds to the colony land contained a dry provision, stipulating that should alcoholic beverages ever be manufactured or dispensed or should premises ever be used as a saloon or for any immoral purposes whatever, then title became null and void and reverted to the Salvation Army.[48] Nels Erikson pointed out that he and Thomas Holland had framed this clause originally, and it carried the specific approval of evangelist Billy Sunday.[49]

The stipulation eventually caused trouble. Under California law, certain types of corporations were prohibited from investing in or making loans on property subject to conditions or right of re-entry. Hence in 1934, because of the liquor clause, the Federal Land Bank of Berkeley could not make loans to Alfreso and Ernastina Nicola of Soledad, holders of some of the old Fort Romie land. The problem arose again five years later when Edwin Handley applied to the Bank of America for a loan on Fort Romie property brought together from colonist holdings. In both instances, Salvation Army leaders were unwilling to abandon the "morality clause" as a matter of course, but would agree to enter into a Subordination Agreement, "subordinating the forfeiture right and reversion of title in the event of manufacture or sale of intoxicating liquor, etc. to the lien of any bonafide mortgage or deed of trust."[50] Thus were principle and practicality accommodated.

CHAPTER NINE

All the World
a Battlefield

*... The scheme which I have evolved, namely, that the Public
Credit & the waste forces of Benevolence can be made use of to
palliate the gigantic evil of the over-crowded cities and to
populate the deserted or unoccupied land....*[1]

THE FIRST FEW YEARS of the new century had seemed to be halcyon
times for the colonial experiment. Editors waxed eloquent over the
Colorado settlement: "Amity! The Prairie Queen!," "A Community of
Plod, Pluck, Perseverance and Peace—The Mecca of the Workless
Workingman." Some writers viewed General Booth's *In Darkest England* as "a marvelous contribution—both theoretical and practical,—to
the diagnosis of modern poverty and to its remedial treatment" and
saw the American colonies as the spiritual heirs of the General's ideas,
yet entirely independent, and as the products of the great energy and
organizing genius of Commander Booth-Tucker.[2] Brigadier Pebble's
"Colonization Song," sung to the tune "Under the Bamboo Tree,"
expressed the same general opinions in different form.

> *The landless man and manless land,*
> *To landless, manless gold;*
> *Forming to-day a trinity*
> *of revenues untold.*

Thus saving the man, enriching the land,
And robbing the poorhouse too;
Giving the child, now running wild,
Something that he can do. [3]

With the experiment seemingly vindicated, Booth-Tucker searched for a means of expanding the settlements. From time to time, benefactors had offered the Army private lands for use as colonies—160 acres in 1898, for example, and in 1903 "two most generous donations," one of 50,000 acres, the other of 20,000—but the Army had taken no advantage of those tenders.[4] Amity and Romie had fulfilled "our most sanguine expectations," the Commander reported, and the families "are entirely self-supporting." But the "one stumbling block" was the lack of capital. What little there was was expensive, came "in driblets," and was of necessity thinly spread "over a considerable area and a long interval of time."[5] The solution, as Booth-Tucker saw it, was to tap the resources of the national government.

The time was ripe. The Newlands Reclamation Act of 1902 had authorized federal reclamation reservoirs in the West; such projects were to be financed by land sales in eleven western states and territories. Public lands in tracts of not over 160 acres were reserved for settlers in the projects. Colonization—especially what he called "scientific colonization"—would prove "a most valuable handmaiden to irrigation," Booth-Tucker argued. The federal government was investing $2 million to put water on the land; it was even more important that it spend a corresponding amount to plant settlers on it.[6]

In September 1903 the Commander attended the Eleventh National Irrigation Congress in Ogden, Utah. On the morning of September 16, he spoke to a subgroup of engineers on colonization; later in the day in what his wife called a "star speech" and what he referred to as "a wonderful triumph for colonization," he made the general case for government support before the full assembly.[7] His experiences in India, he told the gathering, had familiarized him with the positive consequences of irrigation to small farmers—"a nation of market gardeners one might almost call them." The Indian population automatically flowed to occupy free space, but the American West was different. There, settlement required guidance. Large, expensive irrigation projects required quick and full land occupancy to succeed. In the past, settlement of irrigated lands had been almost entirely limited to farmers with beginning capital. Now, for mutual benefit, systematic and scientific colonization was vital to the opening of soon-to-be-watered western lands. The Salvation Army efforts had broken ground: in the Colorado and California colonies, "every family is entirely self-supporting, and the repayments have amounted to considerably more than $20,000."[8]

With capital scarce, Booth-Tucker looked to the federal government to underwrite large scale colonization, though he emphasized again that good business, not merely charity, was involved. To settle 2000 people on either of the major tracts that had been offered to the Army would require about $500,000, an amount far beyond its means. Colonization strengthened the family, argued the Commander, agreeing with Theodore Roosevelt that the large family was most important to national well-being and that its destruction, *domicide*, was one of the worst attributes of modern society. How much better it would be, he said, to expend $50 million a year in moving worthy families onto irrigated farms than to pour an equal amount into urban poverty relief. At that rate, in ten years, at a cost of $500 million, five million people could be made self-sufficient on twenty-five million acres. Colonization was as imperative as irrigation, and it was up to Congress to "throw wide open before our working classes that door of opportunity."[9]

After Booth-Tucker sat down to "a great ovation," as he called it, one of the delegates was supposed to have told a well-known millionaire who was present: "I was expecting you, Senator, to rise and promise a big donation to the Salvation Army." The capitalist in question replied that he was waiting for Senator William Clark of Montana to lead the way, whereupon Emma Booth-Tucker vowed to go after Clark for colony funds or for contributions to a new university scheme the Army was considering.[10]

The Commander's address at Ogden lacked specific details. But he had already passed along the particulars of a definite proposition to Secretary of State John Hay, himself a donor, who promised to bring it to the attention of President Roosevelt. These ideas had been incorporated into a bill which Senator Mark Hanna of Ohio had been persuaded to introduce into Congress, but Hanna had died before he could do so.[11] Hanna was indeed a friend; so much so that the Salvation Army honored him in a special memorial service at their Fourteenth Street Hall in New York.[12]

Subsequently, in March 1904 Senator George Hoar of Massachusetts introduced the bill, a proposal, he said, brought forward at the Commander's request and prepared with the advice and approval of Hanna. The measure would create a federal colonization bureau, headed by a commissioner attached to the Department of the Interior. The United States Government would provide loans of from $500 to $1,500 in cash or materials and in addition forty acres of irrigated or eighty acres of nonirrigated land to each poor but worthy family to settle them on the public domain. Funding would be done by the issuance of sixty-year government gold bonds bearing three percent interest to a total amount of $50 million, with not more than $5 million to be issued in any one year.[13] Booth-Tucker's original proposal to President Roosevelt suggested explicitly that the Salvation Army be made the government's instrument of colonization of 100,000 acres, and the Army would undertake this task without compensation as part of its social work.[14] Whether this was spelled out in the "Booth-Tucker Bill," as some called it, is not clear; certainly it was implicit.

The bill was read twice in the Senate and referred to the Committee on Public Lands, where it apparently ultimately died. But meanwhile, the press around the country aired it widely. The editor of *Technical World* thought the idea "one of the most important movements of the age"; the *Atlanta Constitution* called it "the biggest piece of real charity ever undertaken in the United States." Labor groups in New York, Utica, Rochester, Columbus, Cincinnati, and Louisville all gave it their unanimous endorsement. On the other hand, mild critics thought the idea smacked of paternalism; and some, especially the Denver *Field and Farm* were openly hostile, referring to it as "a skin-grafting game" in which westerners in general were not interested.[15]

Booth-Tucker expanded his arguments in favor of the bill, pointing with pride to the Army's successes with limited resources in Colorado and California. Congress might profit from studying the New Zealand example, he suggested. Over an eight-year period that government had spent $18 million on loan subsidies to settle small holders on their own farms, a program with no losses; indeed, it showed a surplus of $340,000, plus a sinking fund of $600,000.[16] The Commander had talked with Earl Grey in London about proposals for colonies in Canada, Australia, and South Africa, to be funded by bond issues, and had received encouraging responses. As vice president of the British Chartered Company of South Africa, Grey had urged the raising of capital to help settle Rhodesia; and the late Cecil Rhodes himself had earlier evidenced interest in the Army's rural settlement plans. In India, government had invested $125 million in irrigation and colonization, benefiting 800,000 people on newly watered lands. In the American West, where the proposal was to gradually bring some 100 million acres under irrigation, the "Booth-Tucker bill" offered a superb opportunity for a massive federal-private undertaking for social improvement. If nations spent hundreds of millions of dollars putting vast military forces in the field, Booth-Tucker argued, "there is no reason at all why armies of colonists should not be marched ten thousand, twenty thousand, fifty thousand at a time, carefully selected, thoroughly prepared, trained for the object, and settled upon the land in happy, self-supporting communities."[17]

Congress was not receptive. It did not even discuss the bill, which remained bottled up in committee. The scene soon shifted. The locale and the proposed sponsoring government changed, but the philosophy did not. The Salvation Army thus became the projected administrator of a giant colonization scheme focusing on the settlement of British poor on Canadian soil. This, of course, was a logical part of General Booth's original plan in *In Darkest England*—the creation of the "Over-Sea Colony." Frederick Booth-Tucker took an active role in formulating and advocating the new proposal; and the American colonies—his colonies—provided living examples for the Army's efforts to convince Parliament of the desirability of underwriting the settlement program.

In this attempt, the key role was played by H. Rider Haggard, British novelist, gentleman farmer, and sympathetic exponent of the Army concept that the rural flow into the city constituted one of society's worst ills, a theme he had expounded in an earlier book, *Rural England*. In mid-January 1905 Haggard was approached by Alfred Lyttelton, Secretary of State for the colonies, asking if he would accept a commission to inspect and report upon the Salvation Army colonies in California, Colorado, and Ohio.

> It is thought that if on inquiry this sytem is found to be financially sound and to be a real benefit to the poorer classes, it might prove a useful model for some analogous system of settlement from the United Kingdom to the Colonies.[18]

"As an observer both of men and agricultural affairs," Haggard was the logical choice, Lyttelton insisted, adding that Booth-Tucker had advised making the trip early in the year in order to meet settlers "before the strenuous agricultural operations have commenced."[19] Expenses would be drawn from £300 granted by the Rhodes Trustees, who had suggested the inquiry and the appointment of a commissioner. Lyttelton was reported to have agreed, but stipulated sarcastically that public money not be involved:

> You may have your Commission, if you will pay his expenses, for the British Imperial Government has not a sixpence to spare for such trivial questions as those affecting the welfare of millions of our poor.[20]

Haggard's official commission was specific. It urged him "to pay special attention to the class of persons taken by the Salvation Army, their training and success as agricultural settlers, and the general effect upon character and social happiness: you should also consider the financial aspect of the experiments." Once having visited the colonies, Haggard was to proceed to Ottawa for a discussion of colonization with interested officials, especially Lord Grey, who had shown a personal interest and who had been impressed with the Army's work.[21]

Lord Grey expressed delight with Haggard's forthcoming visit and informed him that he had his support and that of Clifford Sifton, his Minister of the Interior. If Haggard's American report was favorable, Sifton could submit to his colleagues a bill "like that drafted by the late Marc Hanna." But this, Grey noted, was not for public consumption.[22] Haggard also cabled his friend, Rudyard Kipling, in South Africa and received a cryptic response:

> What is the telegram about your going out to America to study Salvation Army methods of planting folk on the land with a view to applying 'em to this part of the world? If its' true, hurry up and turn the current this way. We want *picked* men badly, and breeding women worse.[23]

Haggard also contacted Frederick Russell Burnham, another friend from earlier visits in Africa, who was then living in Pasadena, California, and who offered to show him that settlement, one of the first colonies established in the state. "It might shed some light on the very problem you have to solve," the flamboyant Burnham said.[24]

Escorted by Booth-Tucker, Haggard made "a long and searching inspection of the Hadleigh colony in Essex; subsequently had a lengthy interview with General Booth; and on February 22 sailed for New York on the *Teutonic*, accompanied by his daughter, Angela, who served as his private secretary. In Philadelphia, he inspected sites for summer gardens for the poor sponsored by the Vacant Lots Association, a project which he found unimpressive because it was straightforward charity.[25] In Washington, he dined with the British Ambassador, heard engineer F. W. Newell of the new Reclamation Service explain the government's expanding irrigation and land distribution system, discussed with Secretary of Agriculture James Wilson the details of colonization, and "could discover no point of difference between Mr. Wilson's views and my own."[26] At the White House, Haggard met with President Theodore Roosevelt and aired his views on such topics as the Boer War, family limitation, and "matters connected with the land and with the absolute necessity of keeping the population on the soil and not allowing it to flock into the cities." The two found their ideas remarkably compatible; Roosevelt expressed a keen interest in Haggard's mission and asked to be kept informed when the colony investigation was complete.[27]

Traveling to California via the Southern Pacific Railroad, with a three-day delay and "a narrow escape" because of the raging Colorado River at Yuma, Haggard visited Burnham at Pasadena, spoke to 3,000 university students at Berkeley (General "Chinese" Gordon, Cecil Rhodes, and General William Booth were "three of the greatest names in modern history," he told them) and arrived at Fort Romie on March 26 to spend the next two days viewing the colony and interviewing settlers and Army officials.[28]

Quickly Haggard was en route east, enjoying the luxury of the private railway car of an old friend, mining engineer John Hays Hammond, at least part of the way. At Salt Lake City he met with the President and other officials of the Mormon Church to learn more about their small-farm settlers.[29] At Fort Amity, where he was joined by Commander Booth-Tucker on April 5, he spent three more days of inspection and interviewing. There his daughter made a splendid impression: "her cordial and gracious manner at once put all her guests at their ease." Haggard himself was feted and dined, with Denver newspapers headlining his visit in optimistic terms: "Great English Novelist Declares That the Salvation Army Has Gone a Long Way Toward Solving the Problem Presented by the Congested Cities of the World—People Must Return to the Land."[30]

By April 10, Haggard was in Ohio, inspecting the third colony, Fort Herrick, even though it now focused on the settlement of inebriates. Finally, in keeping with his charge from the colonial office, he traveled to Ottawa to confer with Canadian officials, bringing them a rough draft of his report written aboard eastbound trains. Haggard and his daughter were guests of Governor-General Grey at Government House, with entree to other influential officials, including Sir Wilfrid Laurier, the Prime Minister; former Minister of the Interior Clifford Sifton; and Superintendent of Immigration W. D. Scott. At a luncheon honoring him and Booth-Tucker, who had made the trip with him, Haggard spoke to 400 members of the Canadian Club on question of land settlement.[31]

In a more practical move, he bluntly asked the governor-general and the prime minister for a sizeable grant of land. His appraisal of the Salvation Army colonies in the United States was favorable. Would the Government of the Dominion be prepared to donate "a suitable tract" of 240,000 acres, upon which to settle carefully selected poor British families? In addition, would the Dominion help guarantee the interest on a loan to provide the necessary capital to put the colonization scheme into operation? With Earl Grey, the governor-general, leading the way, the government agreed to set aside the requested amount of land—ten full townships. This was to provide homesteads for colonists to be selected by Haggard or any commissioner appointed by His Majesty's Government, subject only to the stipulation that Canadian laws be observed and that school lands and those of the Hudson Bay

Company be exempted. On the other hand, while its land offer was generous, the Dominion Government would make no further financial commitment to provide or underwrite loans to put the colonization scheme into operation.[32] Soon Haggard was en route home to England, pleased with his Ottawa accomplishments, encouraged that a workable plan could be put before Parliament, and no doubt heartened by Earl Grey's parting telegram.

> May the Report you take home weave Canada closer than ever into one piece with England & be the means of providing happy homes for thousands of the worthy disinherited who without hope throng the city life of Great Britain.[33]

Booth-Tucker also returned to England to aid the campaign. It was he who prepared the cost estimates for the proposed colonization in Canada. Haggard believed that it was important to develop greater Canadian input, and he advised using the expertise of outgoing Minister of the Interior Sifton, who viewed the plan "as an embodiment of the truest and best form of Imperial patriotism, because it is building for the future by helping to give a solid British basis to the population of our great West."[34] Sifton had volunteered to sit on a committee to expedite the scheme. Privately Earl Grey believed that it would be good strategy for the home government to refer Haggard's report to Ottawa for response but that it was necessary to hurry. "As you know I agree entirely with you that there is no time to lose — Roosevelt will be glad to blanket our sails if we give him an opportunity."[35]

Even before his report was formally presented to Parliament, Haggard sent a copy to President Roosevelt, seeking his reaction but cautioning confidentiality until the colonial office formally released the publication a fortnight or so later. In response, Roosevelt extolled the advantage of business principles over mere charity, but seemed wary of becoming involved:

> I could say nothing of value to you for quotation, but I trust I need hardly say that I agree absolutely with your purpose and with the general outline of your plan; although I am not sufficiently familiar with the subject to speak as to the details.[36]

Haggard's report, with accompanying documents, was issued in bluebook form under the title *Report on the Salvation Army Colonies in the United States and at Hadleigh, England, with Scheme of National Land Settlement* (Cd. 2562), and was presented to both Houses of Parliament in June 1905. It used the experiments at Fort Romie and Fort Amity as precedents, as it were, for a much larger scheme based upon the

240,000 acres pledged by Canadian officials. Haggard now proposed the raising of £300,000, the interest on which was to be guaranteed by the British Home Government or jointly with the colonial governments involved; he advocated per capita contributions from Poor Law Authorities in large English cities for every family taken off their local rolls for colonization. He also called for the selection of a permanent superintendent of land settlement, to take care of the settling of the first 1,500 families in Canada and of subsequent endeavors. Haggard urged that the Salvation Army be delegated the tasks of selecting, distributing, and organizing colonists on lands anywhere in the British Empire, with a special look at South Africa. Should his report receive a favorable verdict, Haggard believed that a "National Land Settlements Act" in Parliament was the next logical step. It was his opinion that "the future welfare of this country," and indeed of the United States as well, "depends upon whether or not it is possible to retain or to settle upon the soil a fair proportion of its, or their, inhabitants."[37]

Fully half of the report was devoted to the American colonies, with which he was "on the whole extremely well satisfied." Admitting that the Army had lost some £10,000 due to drought at Romie, to the high cost of land and of borrowing, to the undercharging of settlers for their land, and to the unexpected cost of handling alkali at Fort Amity, Haggard believed that both represented success "very cheaply bought." There would be no repetition of these difficulties, and critics were wrong to label them "financially a failure."[38]

As might be expected, Salvation Army publications on both sides of the Atlantic were enthusiastic about this "Momentous Blue Book," this "Splendid Report," which constituted "an unsought, official, and unanswerable testimonial to the practical wisdom of the General's plans, as foreshadowed in 'In Darkest England.'" At the end of the year, the London edition of *The War Cry* called Haggard's report "one of the events of 1905." At first, the leading newspapers in England gave an excellent press, with wide coverage and a not unsympathetic hearing. The *Times*, for example although doubtful of enriching the Colonies with the best of Britain's rural stock, devoted three-and-a-half columns to the report in one issue.[39]

Despite the spritely discussions in the summer of 1905, it was clear that not everyone agreed. Perhaps it was this early opposition that prompted Haggard to publish a slightly expanded version of the report as *The Poor and the Land*, in which he included an introduction which tried to refute, point by point, the criticisms that were in the air. He also added more than a dozen pages of press opinions, all favorable, at the end.

In a long interview with Lord Rosebery, Haggard suggested that the scheme be brought before the House of Lords, but before any action could be taken, Secretary of State Lyttelton announced that the report would be put into the hands of a nine-man departmental committee, chaired by Lord Tennyson.[40]

Matters moved slowly. Earl Grey wrote from Canada that the Provincial Parliament would probably not deal with the issue during the current session. Grey also expressed sorrow that the so-called "Booth-Tucker Bill," written by Mark Hanna, had not been included in the bluebook report. "I regret its absence," he said, "as it gives a lead and shows the way."[41] As early as August, Bramwell Booth noted that his father, the General, was disappointed by the inaction of the Tennyson committee and the seeming unwillingness to consult Canadians about the success of colonizing men from English cities on the prairies. The younger Booth confided to Haggard: "It would appear that in some way there is a wish to set up y^r Report in order to shoot at it! ... My own feeling is that Gov^t had really ceased any serious intention in this matter—they are practically in a state of suspended animation."[42]

Moving at its own pace, the Committee held twenty-one meetings in the fall of 1905 and examined forty-one witnesses, including Haggard and Booth-Tucker. Haggard later insisted that General William Booth was so incensed at the attitude toward the report that he refused to appear to give evidence. "Indeed his people would not allow him to do so," said Haggard, "because they said they were sure that he would lose his temper."[43] Most of the testimony came from spokesmen of other charitable groups or of emigration agencies, ranging from the Church Army and the Turnbridge Wells Colonisation Association to the Liverpool Self-Help Emigration Society and the Waifs and Strays Society.

In the end, after careful examination of the evidence, whether looking at Canada, South Africa, or Australia, the committee failed "to find an instance of a thoroughly successful effort at colonisation." While lauding Haggard's zeal and good intentions, it was

> ... obliged to say that we consider his scheme to be so open to so many objections, that even if we were prepared to advocate colonisation in principle, we could not recommend that this particular scheme should be adopted.[44]

The Committee found Haggard's arguments less than persuasive. The proposed colony was too large; the expense of settling it was underestimated; difficulties of selection of settlers were understated; returns were uncertain; settlement of men without colonial experience was unwise; and management by a religious body was undesirable. Moreover, the American precedents of Amity and Romie were "inapplicable." Their colonists were already residents of the country and many had farm experience; their numbers were too small to have any meaning for an enterprise involving 1,500 families spread over 300 square miles; the prairies of northwestern Canada presented conditions far different from those in irrigated California and Colorado; even the financial success at Romie and Amity, said the Committee, "is by no means insured." Thus the recommendation was for no action "to further any scheme of colonisation" but instead to encourage emigration of individuals.[45]

Although writers for the popular press or even in scholarly journals often approved of the Committee's action, Haggard found it disappointing and short-sighted. In part he blamed "bitter prejudice against the Salvation Army, often enough fostered by persons in religion who should know better." He agreed with General Booth that the committee was "a put-up job," and that it had unfairly heard testimony from self-interested representatives of English emigration agencies but none from Canadians. Most of all, Haggard believed that his proposal had been scuttled by a lack of high-level leadership. Prime Minister Balfour, he had been informed by Lyttelton, would not even read the report. As Haggard later put it, a strong man, such as Joseph Chamberlain in his prime,

> . . . might have adopted the outline of my ideas and made something of them. But the strong man was lacking, and to send them to a hybrid Committee of mixed views was only to ensure their murder.[46]

The conservative Balfour government was not interested in state interference; rather it espoused the self-help doctrine so familiar to the pre-World War Anglo-American world. And Haggard concluded pessimistically: "But so it is, and so I suppose it will go on—the devouring cities growing more and more bloated, and the starved land becoming more and more empty."[47]

Haggard may not have been soothed by the words of the American Ambassador to Great Britain, Whitelaw Reid, who had read the colony report and expressed the hope that

> . . . the insane rush to the cities will be diminished a little by several causes now beginning to operate. Such colonies as you propose ought to succeed. Then the easy diffusion of electrical energy for light manufacturing ought to scatter the congestion in some of the poorest city districts. Motor buses, & motor cars have their part to play, too, in making the country more accessible for the poor and more attractive to the rich.[48]

At least Haggard had the satisfaction in mid-March 1907 of seeing off from Euston Station in London "a highly respectable body of emigrants," nearly 1000 strong, selected by the Salvation Army, and en route to Liverpool and Canada. The Army, he noted, had arranged to send 20,000 to Canada that year, not as colonists, but as individual emigrants. Less than two weeks later, Haggard was writing his friend in California, Fred Burnham, to ask if he would go to Mexico to inspect the site for a colony to be managed by two Salvation Army officers if it materialized.[49]

Thus Booth-Tucker had failed in his efforts to convince the American Congress to subsidize colonization experiments in the West on a grand scale. Likewise, his—and Haggard's—effort to use Fort Amity and Romie as precedents for massive colony efforts, underwritten by the governments of Britain and Canada, were not successful. In 1903, according to Booth-Tucker, the Army had established several farm colonies in South Africa, not as ongoing back-to-the land settlements like those in Colorado and California, but temporary work situations for stranded and needy whites. A tract of 3,000 acres had been given to the Army in Rhodesia, and two comparable expanses in Zululand for the organization of native settlements had "made considerable progress" in spite of the Boer War.[50]

About the same time, it was announced that General William Booth had purchased 3,000 acres in Liberia for an industrial settlement where native Salvation Army officers would be trained to spread the Gospel.[51] In 1906, it was reported that the British South Africa Company had offered the Army one million free acres in Rhodesia, with the stipulation that if colonization failed, the land reverted to the company. Booth admitted "a certain amount of truth" to the report, but that it was yet premature. The General referred to this as the greatest colonization proposal "since Moses left Egypt," but nothing came of it. Shareholders of the British South African Company failed to respond to an appeal for fresh capital, and in early 1908 the colony plan was abandoned.[52]

Early in the century some 20,000 acres had been turned over to the Salvation Army by the Australian Government. Located in Western Australia, 125 miles from Perth, the land was valued at eight shillings an acre and was to be paid for over a twenty-year period. It was to be used for colonization and for children's homes, but there is little evidence that it was developed.[53]

In India, however, the Army was to establish a number of farm colonies, although of a type different from those at Amity and Romie. After a brief stint in England, Booth-Tucker remarried and in 1907 returned to India, where he organized several agricultural settlements for criminal tribes in the Punjab, Gujerat, and Travancore, twenty-seven of them by 1915.[54] But these were designed as work farms for the needy or undesirable or as models for the teaching of better farm techniques; they were not outlets for the urban poor as Amity and Romie were conceived to be.

When Parliament rejected Haggard's plan, the Salvation Army abandoned the concept of the back-to-the land colony in favor of a vigorous promotion of emigration, particularly to Canada. In early February 1905, it was reported that already 1,200 settlers had been sent to Canada and that the Dominican liner *Vancouver* had been chartered to carry another group. Soon, after addresses by Booth-Tucker, Mrs. Bramwell Booth, H. Rider Haggard, and the Lord Mayor of Liverpool, the *Vancouver* steamed out of the harbor, the Salvation Army flag at her masthead, carrying 1,045 emigrants. Bramwell Booth later reported that during the first six months of 1905, the Army had placed 3,256 people in Canada, 90 percent of them in agriculture-connected work.[55]

By the end of December, the Army had opened an office on Queen Victoria Street in London for its emigration work—"The Poor Man's 'Cook and Sons'!," *The War Cry* called it.[56] Within a year, its emigration department was publishing regularly the *Emigration Gazette*, a London promotional magazine which focused mainly on migration to Canada. Between 1906 and 1909, a period of relatively high unemployment in England, the Salvation Army sent more than 50,000 to work for Canadian farmers, in lumber camps, and on railroad construction crews.[57] They were not colonists in the old sense, but many did eventually take up homesteads and become the kind of small farm-holders that General Booth and Booth-Tucker had envisioned on a large scale.

For all practical purposes, the rejection of Haggard's proposal in 1906 spelled the end of the Salvation Army's hopes for a successful farm-colony program. Without substantial expansion, which could only come from the government, or possibly from an extremely wealthy benefactor, Amity and Romie were mere experiments, small ripples in a sea of poverty—just as Holland and Booth-Tucker always insisted they were. Too few people were involved in both instances. And even at the California colony, it is not certain that the beneficiaries were hard-core urban poor. Rather the second wave—the post 1901 group—seem to have been country folk; to be sure, they were country folk struggling to make a living.

To American society in general, the colonization scheme was attractive. Not only would it remove the poor from overcrowding, depression, and unemployment, it would automatically "better the condition of the manufacturer, and advance the whole nation commercially, morally and intellectually."[58] But there was a wide gap between vocal support and monetary support, especially when the colonies were small and the outcome uncertain. More than once, Booth-Tucker reported that men of influence (and affluence) had made it clear that the success of Amity or Romie was the key to much larger contributions.

The Army was aware of this and realized how important the colonies were to the image of the organization, and recognized the potential they held for attracting funds. "Some of the finest business men and minds and some of the deepest thinkers" in America believe "we shall have more money left to our colonization plan than to any other existing philanthropy," wrote Booth-Tucker in 1902. The scheme had tremendous potential. As former Secretary of the Navy Benjamin Tracy, a staunch supporter, once remarked of the western colonization plan: "What a plank for a political platform!"[59]

But the major breakthrough never came. There was no opportunity for expansion. Begun with limited funds, the American colonies were put on firmer foundations with the bond issue of 1901, but they were never duplicated or projected on a more extensive basis. When pressed, Thomas Holland defended them as pilot endeavors, to determine whether the urban poor could indeed be happy and successful in a rural setting. But without additional funding, private or governmental, the dream of three million needy "waiting to be led into their modern Canaan" remained unfulfilled.[60]

The charge that colonists failed because they lacked agricultural experience is largely unfounded. While those in the first wave at Fort Romie were soon vanquished, who could say that it was a lack of farming skill rather than the drought that brought their downfall? With the fresh start of 1901, both more-seasoned farmers and an adequate irrigation system were introduced. Booth-Tucker did admit that too many inexperienced people had been selected at Amity: "We went too far down that 'lane'; we took too large a proportion of the non-agriculturists." In the future, he recommended in 1905, at least two-thirds ought to have some knowledge of farming.[61] At Amity, of course, as was detailed earlier, the basic flaw that subverted the entire operation was the failure to understand irrigation and the need for drainage to prevent salinity in the soil. A career of farm experience in nonirrigated Ohio or Illinois would hardly have prevented that particular difficulty. And the seeming ineffectiveness of the drainage program conceived by experts provided the final impetus to disintegration of the colony.

If the Army was correct in its belief that one of its most important contributions to the cause of colonization was leadership, then the accidental death of Consul Emma Booth-Tucker may have dealt the crippling blow to Fort Amity. As a writer for the *The War Cry* phrased it later, "On her return journey the Angel of Death opened the switch and she went bounding on to the city of the New Jerusalem, instead of Chicago...."[62] Emma's death was a shattering blow to Booth-Tucker, now left with six children, all under the age of thirteen. In June 1904, he spoke in Carnegie Hall on his favorite topic, "The Landless Man to the Manless Land," but the fire seemed to have gone out of his work; soon he left for London and a new assignment. With the Consul dead, Booth-Tucker gone and Secretary Thomas Holland in poor health, the mainsprings of the American farm colony movement had been removed, just at a time when Amity was about to face its most serious crisis.[63]

As indicated earlier, the Army colonies were not isolated phenomena. They were a logical part of an ongoing back-to-the-land movement which waned in times of prosperity and expanded in times of depression. The twentieth century, especially, would bring forth numerous kindred experiments and ardent proponents who must have agreed wholeheartedly with the Army's approach. For example, one who had wide influence in the movement was Bolton Hall, whose practical little books, *Three Acres and Liberty* and *A Little Land and a Living*, brimmed with advice and echoed at least part of General William Booth's philosophy: "Most sociologists are agreed that the great problem of our day is to stop the drift of population toward the cities."[64]

The readers of such books might follow with considerable interest the fate of not only Fort Amity and Fort Romie, but also of other more private agricultural colonies that followed. They would no doubt have been familiar with William E. Smythe, who devoted much of his adult life to "the conquest of arid America," as he called the combination of irrigation and colonization, and who constantly waxed eloquent over reclamation of the desert, sounding much like Booth-Tucker when he argued that irrigation was "a religious rite" and that the man who farmed with irrigation was certainly "an instrument in the process of evolution."[65]

Earlier, Smythe had been instrumental in organizing a successful Idaho colony, New Plymouth, with most of the settlers urban and professional people from Chicago and the Midwest, not city poor. He was also responsible for the Little Landers movement, beginning in 1908, when he founded San Ysidro, south of San Diego, the first of three California settlements based on the idea that, properly organized and instructed, a family could live a decent rural life on from one to five acres—a premise which proved untrue in these instances because of a variety of problems.[66]

Interested observers would also have noted that in 1910 the governor and other Missouri state officials were pushing a plan to colonize large tracts in Texas, Missouri, Louisiana, Alabama, and other states with "utopian clusters of farmers," through a new National Farm Homes Association, which with funds from philanthropists, hoped to buy land, improve it, and stock it with both livestock and settlers, again reminiscent of the Salvation Army plan.[67] Informed readers might have taken note of the Jewish Agricultural and Colonial Society, a Philadelphia agency organized to send settlers to settle lands in Utah in 1912 and 1913. With funds raised by small investors, the Society sent fifty families the first year, each with house, forty acres, and generous monetary advance. Another 100 families were contemplated for the spring of 1913, to be financed by a $150,000 bond issue, a feature resembling of the Army's 1901 financial arrangements.[68]

Another back-to-the-land group in the public limelight prior to World War I was the National Forward to the Land League, organized in 1911 by Haviland H. Lund and his wife to put the urban poor on farms. Both staunch conservatives, the Lunds believed that private colonization was needed to protect the nation from the "red virus" which they saw as a threat on every side. Through leaflets, lectures by farm specialists and lobbying in Congress and in the Republican party, they worked for years without practical results and in the end blamed the radicals who had permeated national government.[69]

And no one concerned with colonization or resettlement efforts in the early twentieth century could have been unaware of Elwood Mead, best known as the director of the Bureau of Reclamation when Hoover Dam was built. A civil engineer and one of the world's leading irrigation authorities, between 1907 and 1915 Mead supervised reclamation and the settlement of thirty-two government irrigation projects in Australia. He returned to head the California Commission on Colonization and Rural Credits, convinced that private colonization was generally unworkable. Like Booth-Tucker, he believed that capital and credit were the keys to farm ownership. Without them, he said, "the cry of 'Back to the Land' is a delusion or a fraud." He deemed government support vital and was delighted in 1917 when the California legislature followed his recommendation and passed the first land settlement law in the country, a statute under which the state bought unimproved lands, divided them into small allotments, built roads and water systems, and granted low-interest, long-term loans to "worthy landless" buyers to create two highly publicized colonies, Durham, which was reasonably successful, and Delhi, which proved to be a financial disaster.[70] Here was a rare, or probably unique, application of a version of the "Booth-Tucker bill" of 1904 at a state level.

Before the results had been finally tabulated, Mead and William E. Smythe had thrown their support behind Secretary of the Interior Franklin Lane's effort to put World War I veterans onto the unoccupied lands. From 1916 through 1923 there was always at least one such colonization bill in Congress. "Let's give each returning soldier a farm," rang the popular cry, with supporters pointing out that Canada,

New Zealand, Australia, Canada, and the Union of South Africa were all lending aid to such ex-servicemen's benefits. Most of these measures were cooperative in design, with states to provide land and the federal government to advance funds for irrigation, drainage, or clearance and for preparation for planting, including implements, livestock, and seed. But despite enthusiastic discussion and enactment of laws by twenty-three states (most except California's hinging on federal action), Capitol Hill passed nothing, probably because of American legislators' deep-seated distaste for government intervention in areas long considered the private sector and because the wartime boom continued until 1921 and the recession that followed was much more severe for agriculture than for industry.[71]

But, ironically, even in the twenties, a time of stagnation and low farm income, rural folk still sang their praises of the land. With the general crash that commenced in 1929, the back-to-the-farm movement gained new ground everywhere. The lean years of the early thirties saw more urban migration to the country than ever before in American history. Spontaneously, without regulation or direction, often with little hope and even less farming experience, desperate city people squatted on land, moved in with kinfolk, bought or rented small plots, and read how-to-do-it accounts by Ralph Borsodi or E. M. Kains.[72] There was more discussion and more crackpot schemes than ever before, too, which prompted one skeptic to write: "The march back home moves to a various inner music, as profound and cleansing as the psalm beginning, 'The Lord is My Shepherd,' and as noisily self-deceptive as a mammy song."[73]

The Pingree vacant-lot garden idea was revived, with Henry Ford sponsoring 50,000 of them in Detroit and requiring all employees in his Iron Mountain plant to grow vegetables—"Henry Ford's Shotgun Gardens," the *Washington News* called them.[74] William Randolph Hearst urged his newspaper readers to "Get Back to the Earth"; physical culturist Bernarr MacFadden preached the same message, and his lobbyists pushed for congressional legislation to aid getting the unemployed back on the farm.[75] Church groups, especially the Catholics, often influenced by the "distributionism" of Hilaire Belloc, philosophical disciples of Rousseau or Thoreau, city planners seeking to implement Ebenezer Howard's concept of the garden-city idea, old-fashioned agrarians rejecting modernity, following the call of Twelve Southerners in *I'll Take My Stand*, and a variety of anti-capitalists, decentralists, and socialists all took up the call for directed programs of land settlement. Here, one called for a colony to be established in each state, using the expertise of the Bureau of Reclamation and the Department of Agriculture and funds from the Federal Land Bank. There, another proposed an agricultural army, to enlist families, build log houses, and produce food and clothing for their own consumption.[76] And in the midst of all these suggestions, Representative Fiorello LaGuardia of New York reported that the Salvation Army had turned back the calendar and was planning to move several thousand city unemployed to unoccupied farms in the country, a program which apparently was never begun because of a lack of funds.[77]

In the end, after several resettlement bills—now labeled subsistence homesteads bills—had been ignored by the New Deal Congress, in 1933, with White House support, a successful amendment tacked on the National Industrial Recovery Act gave the Roosevelt administration the needed emergency authorization for a federal program of nearly one-hundred planned resettlement communities, the kind of colonies reformers had been advocating for decades. As indicated by one historian of these New Deal projects, the shaping and direction of these came primarily from social scientists and advocates of government planning, but their creation would have been impossible without the back-to-the-land movement of the depression period."[78] And that movement of the thirties was an intensified extension of a more general trend, of which the Salvation Army and Forts Amity and Romie had been a part. Even so, the vantage point of time and perspective make it clear that the Army's real successes came in the crowded streets and tenements of the urban slums, not in the cultivated fields of rural America.

Although ingenious interpretations of General Booth's *In Darkest England* ideas, Amity, Romie, and Herrick were far from being the Salvation Army's most significant contributions in the pre-World War I era. Its support of emigration to Canada was much more important and touched a far greater number of individual lives. But even more important and successful in the long run was the use of its city agencies to uplift the poor and the unfortunate. If Booth's book had originally motivated the colony plan, it had also given the first great impetus to what Army leaders came to regard as organized warfare against social ills necessary to clear the way for evangelical battle. Down though the years its greatest contributions came through its urban social work—through its maternity homes, rehabilitation centers, shelters for the down-and-out, free employment bureaus, summer camps for women and children, agencies to search for relatives, and Harbor Light corps working among skid-row drunkards. In the end it proved that man could be saved in his urban environment; success here indirectly proved that he need not be transplanted to achieve full potential.

Notes to the Chapters

CHAPTER ONE: A QUIET LIFE IN THE COUNTRY

1. Horace, Epode II, from Sir Walter Scott, ed., *The Works of John Dryden*, 2nd ed. (Edinburgh: Arnold Constable & Co., 1921), 12: 351.
2. Colorado Writers' Project, "The Names of Colorado Towns," *The Colorado Magazine* 17 (January, 1940): 31; Ann B. Fisher, *The Salinas: Upside-down River* (New York and Toronto: Farrar & Rinehart, 1945), p. 259.
3. *An Account of the Poor-Colonies, and Agricultural Workhouses, of the Benevolent Society of Holland* (Edinburgh: printed for Peter Brown & James Duncan, 1828), pp. xi, xiii, 1, 10, 145, 181; Annet Royaard, "Farms for the Country's Poor: Experiments in Which Agriculture is used to Better Humanity," *The Craftsman* 25 (November, 1913): 169–70, 171; J. Howard Gore, "The Poor Colonies of Holland," U.S. Department of Labor *Bulletin* No. 2 (Washington: January, 1896), pp. 113–17; Harold E. Moore, *Back to the Land* (London: Methuen & Co., 1893), pp. 16–18, 19.
4. Louis Napoleon Bonaparte, *Extinction du Paupérisme,* in Charles-Edouard Temblaire, ed., *Oeuvres de Louis-Napoleon Bonaparte* (Paris: Libraire Napoleoninne, 1848), vol. 2, pp. 251–304.
5. Moore, *Back to the Land*, pp. 19–20, 208–10; *An Account of the Poor-Colonies*, 187; *The Chicago Tribune*, July 20, 1902; *Encyclopaedia Britannica*, 14th ed. (New York & Chicago: Encyclopaedia Britannica, Inc., 1936) 9:80.
6. See Chapter 2, p. 10.
7. C. S. Orwin and W. F. Darke, *Back to the Land* (London: P.S. King & Son, Ltd., 1935), 14–16; Frederic Impey, *Three Acres and a Cow* (London: Swan Sonnenschein, Le Bas, & Lowrey, 1885); Moore, *Back to the Land*, 137–143; Charles William Stubbs, *The Land and the Labourers* (London: W. Swan Sonnenschein & Co., 1884), 106–147. Robert England, *The Colonization of Western Canada* (London: P.S. King & Son, Ltd., 1936), pp. 59–60, 62.
8. Isador Singer, ed., *The Jewish Encyclopedia* (New York & London: Funk & Wagnalls Co., 1901) 1: 241–59; Samuel Joseph, *History of the Baron de Hirsch Fund* (Baron de Hirsch Fund, 1935), pp. 8–9, 33.
9. For detailed treatment of these three measures of 1877–1878, see Albert V. House, Jr., "Proposals of Government Aid to Agricultural Settlement During the Depression of 1873–1879," *Agricultural History* 12 (January 1938):46–66.

10. Frederick de Latour Booth-Tucker, "Farm Colonies of the Salvation Army," U.S. Bureau of Labor *Bulletin* 48 (Washington: September 1903), pp. 997—98; cited hereafter as Booth-Tucker, "Farm Colonies" (1). See also Henry Demerest Lloyd, *Newest England: Notes of A Democratic Traveller in New Zealand, With Some Australian Comparisons* (New York: Doubleday, Page & Co., 1900), pp. 159—71, 175, 195—96, 204—5.

11. See John Lancaster Spalding, *The Religious Mission of the Irish People and Catholic Colonization* (New York: Catholic Publication Society Co., 1880), pp. 67—68. Ford, *Writings*, vol. 7, p. 36; Ralph Waldo Emerson, *Society and Solitude* (Boston: Fields, Osgood & Co., 1870), p. 123; *The Writings and Speeches of Daniel Webster* (Boston: Little, Brown & Co., 1903), vol. 2, p. 307.

12. Richard Hofstadter, *The Age of Reform* (New York: Vintage Books, 1961); Leo Marx, *The Machine in the Garden: Technology and the Pastoral Ideal in America* (London, Oxford and New York: Oxford University Press, 1964); Marvin Meyers, *The Jacksonian Persuasion: Politics and Belief* (New York: 1960); Henry Nash Smith, *Virgin Land: The American West as Symbol and Myth* (Cambridge: Harvard University Press and M.I.T. Press, 1950).

13. Robert H. Walker, *The Poet and the Gilded Age* (Philadelphia: University of Pennsylvania Press, 1963), p. 47.

14. Henry George, *Social Problems* (Garden City: Doubleday, Page & Co., 1911), pp. 234—35.

15. "The Road to Boston," in Sam Walter Foss, *Back Country Poems* (Boston: Lee & Shepherd, 1894), p. 27.

16. Booth-Tucker to Herbert Booth, February 2, 1902, copy, Unprocessed National Commander Collection, Salvation Army Archives and Research Center, New York City; cited hereafter as National Commander Collection, SAA.

17. Raymond Philip Witte, *Twenty-five Years of Crusading: A History of the National Catholic Rural Life Conference* (Des Moines: Catholic Rural Life Conference, 1948), pp. 26—27; Spalding, *The Religious Mission*, pp. 174—80, 191, 197.

18. See Robert V. Hine, *California's Utopian Colonies* (San Marino: Huntington Library, 1953); James F. Willard, ed., *The Union Colony at Greeley, Colorado 1869—1871* (Boulder: University of Colorado, 1918); James F. Willard and Colin B. Goodykoontz, eds., University of Colorado, 1926).

CHAPTER TWO: IN DARKEST ENGLAND

1. William Booth, *In Darkest England and the Way Out* (London: The Salvation Army, 1890), p.92.

2. Booth, *In Darkest England*, p. 45; Herbert A. Wisbey, Jr., *Soldiers Without Swords: A History of the Salvation Army in the United States* (New York: Macmillan Co., 1956), p. 17; H. W. C. Davis & J. R. H. Weaver, eds., *The Dictionary of National Biography, 1912—1921* (Oxford: Oxford University Press; London: Humphry Milford, 1927), pp. 50, 51, 52; hereafter cited as *D.N.B., 1912—1921*.

3. Booth, *In Darkest England*, pp. 17, 90, 92.

4. For O'Connor's land colony scheme, see W. H. G. Armytage, "The Chartist Land Colonies 1846—1848," *Agricultural History* 32 (April 1958):87—98 and Donald Read and Eric Glasgow, *Feargus O'Connor: Irishman and Chartist* (London: Edward Arnold, 1961), pp. 108—17.

5. *D.N.B., 1912—1921*, pp. 51, 507—8; William Hamilton Nelson, *Blood & Fire: General William Booth* (New York and London: Century Co., 1929), pp. 211—13, 217.

6. George R. Sims, *et al.*, *Sketches of the Salvation Army Social Work* (London: The Salvation Army, 1906), p. xxi.

7. Booth, *In Darkest England*, pp. 92—93, 94—95, 107, 111—12.

8. *Ibid.*, p. 125.

9. *Ibid.*, pp. 128, 133, 135—37.

10. *Ibid.*, 133−34, 137, 139, 140−41, 142. For the Ralahine cooperative farm experiment in County Clare, see Charles William Stubbs, *The Land and the Labourers* (London: W. Swan Sonnenschein & Co., 1884), pp. 63−106.

11. Quoted in Harold Begbie, *Life of William Booth* (London: Macmillan & Co., 1926), vol. 2, pp. 39, 43.

12. Booth, *In Darkest England*, pp. 143, 145−47, 150, 153−54.

13. *Ibid.*, p. 93.

14. For a general, but by no means comprehensive, discussion of the arguments over the book, see Herman Ausubel, "General Booth's Scheme of Social Salvation," *American Historical Review* 56 (April 1951):521−24.

15. D. Bosanquet, *"In Darkest England" On the Wrong Track* (London: Swan Sonnenschein & Co., 1891), p. 1; Thomas H. Huxley, *Social Diseases and Worse Remedies* (London: Macmillan & Co., 1891), p. 7.

16. R. B. Roxby, *General Booth, Limited* (London: R. Sutton, n.d.), p. 17; Robert Eyton, *A Rash Investment* (London: Kegan Paul, Trench, Trubner & Co., 1890), pp. 1−6; R. W. Dale, *General Booth's Scheme* (Birmingham: Cornish Bros., 1890), pp. 13, 15−16; *Punch* 99 (November 8, 1890): 218; Nelson, *Blood & Fire*, pp. 218−19.

17. Walter Besant, "The Farm and the City," *Contemporary Review* 72 (December 1897):792−802; C. S. Bremner, "Hadleigh Farm Colony," *The Nation* 69 (August 30, 1894):154−55; *Hadleigh: The Story of a Great Endeavor* (St. Albans: The Salvation Army, n.d.); *Illustrated Guide to the Salvation Army Land and Industrial Colony, Hadleigh, Essex* (St. Albans: Campfield Press, n.d.), pp. 1−18; H. Rider Haggard, *Regeneration* (London: Longmans Green & Co., 1910), pp. 194−99; *The Deliverer* 8 (February 1897):307.

CHAPTER THREE:
ORGANIZING THE AMERICAN COLONIES

1. *The War Cry* (SF), July 21, 1900.

2. Robert H. Bremner, *From the Depths: The Discovery of Poverty in the United States* (New York: New York University Press, 1956), p. 69.

3. Richard T. Ely, "Pauperism in the United States," *The North American Review* 152 (April 1891):395.

4. Charles Richmond Henderson, *The Social Spirit in America* (Chicago: Scott, Foresman and Co., 1905), p. 319.

5. Bremner, *From the Depths*, pp. 72, 84−85, 123−25, 131; Sidney Lens, *Poverty: America's Enduring Paradox* (New York: Thomas Y. Crowell Co., 1971), pp. 199−200, 201−3.

6. Wisbey, *Soldiers Without Swords*, pp. 86−87.

7. Harry Williams, *Booth-Tucker: William Booth's First Gentleman* (London, Sydney, Auckland, and Toronto: Hodder & Stoughton, 1980), pp. 71−134; Frederick Arthur Mackenzie, *Booth-Tucker: Sadhu and Saint* (London: Hodder & Stoughton, 1930), pp. 22−147.

8. Mackenzie, *Booth-Tucker*, pp. 151−52; Williams, *Booth-Tucker*, pp. 123−24, 144−45, 162.

9. Williams, *Booth-Tucker*, pp. 31, 160−61; Wisbey, *Soldiers Without Swords*, pp. 121−23, 128.

10. *The War Cry* (SF), February 13 and 20; May 1; July 3, 1897; January 22, 1898.

11. *The War Cry* (SF), January 23, 1897.

12. *Ibid.* For Mayor Hazen Stuart Pingree's garden plan and its spread to other cities, see H. Roger Grant, *Self-Help in the 1890s Depression* (Ames: Iowa State University Press, 1983), pp. 23−40. How much Booth-Tucker knew about the Pingree plan at this point is conjectural. A year later he asked a cohort to investigate the Potato Patch idea, with the possibility of doing "something extensive in this line this summer." Frederick Booth-Tucker to Richard Holz, April 8, 1898, Richard Holz MSS, SAA.

13. Clipping, San Francisco *Report*, March 22, 1897; clipping, San Francisco *Call*, March 23, 1897, both in Scrapbook 2:128–29, John Ephrain Thomas Milsaps Collection, Houston Public Library; *The War Cry* (SF), April 3 and 24, 1897.

14. Wisbey, *Soldiers Without Swords*, p. 89.

15. *The War Cry* (SF), May 29 and June 5, 1897.

16. Frederick Booth-Tucker, "The Farm Colonies of the Salvation Army," *The Forum* 23 (August, 1897):756-57. Cited hereafter as Booth-Tucker, "Farm Colonies" (2); *The War Cry* (SF), July 10 and August 14, 1897.

17. *The War Cry* (SF), May 29 and June 5, 1897.

18. *The War Cry* (SF), June 19; August 14 and 28, 1897.

19. Booth-Tucker, "Farm Colonies" (2), pp. 757–58.

20. *Ibid.*, p. 750.

21. *Ibid.*, p. 754.

22. *Ibid.*, p. 760.

23. U.S. Ms Census of Monterey County, California, 1900; Fisher, *The Salinas*, p. 259.

24. Romie's interest rate was three percent instead of six and payment was to be made in three installments—at the end of four, seven and ten years. *The War Cry* (SF), September 11, 1897.

25. *The War Cry* (SF), September 11, 1897; San Francisco *Bulletin*, September 16, 1897; entries for September 17 and 18, 1897, Diary of John E. T. Milsaps, Milsaps Collection.

26. *San Francisco Examiner*, September 17, 1897.

27. *The War Cry* (SF), August 14, 1897; *The War Cry* (NY), October 16, 1897; Frederick Booth-Tucker, "The Relation of Colonization to Irrigation," *Forestry and Irrigation* 9 (October 1903):500.

28. Denver *Times*, November 30, 1897; *New York Tribune*, November 30 and December 1, 1897; *The War Cry* (NY), December 18, 1897.

29. *New York Tribune*, November 30 and December 1, 1897; Denver *Republican*, December 1, 1897.

30. *The Chicago Times-Herald*, December 13 and 15, 1897; *Salinas Evening Democrat* (Salinas, California), December 8, 1897; Denver *Rocky Mountain News*, January 1, 1899.

31. *The War Cry* (NY), June 11, 1898; November 11, 1899; May 21, 1904.

32. *Rocky Mountain News*, January 1, 1899; H. Rider Haggard, *The Poor and the Land* (London and Bombay: Longmans, Green & Co., 1905), pp. 73–74; Thomas Holland to W. Wiley, September 7, 1898, in *Holly Chieftain* (Holly, Colorado), September 9, 1898.

33. Quoted in *The War Cry* (NY), December 11, 1897.

34. *Holly Chieftain*, November 26, 1897; Denver *Republican*, December 2, 1897.

35. Wisbey, *Soldiers Without Swords*, p. 72; Tucson *Star*, February 11, 1898; *The War Cry* (SF), March 19, 1898; clipping, Williams, Arizona, *News*, January 22, 1898; Scrapbook 2: no page numbers; entries for February 8, 9, and 10, Diary of John E. T. Milsaps, 3 (new series), diary and scrapbook in Milsaps Collection.

36. Wilbur Gale to Richard E. Holz, May 4, 1898, Fort Herrick Files (Ac. 82–75), SAA; Gale to Holz, May 10, 1898, Holz MSS, SAA; Allen Johnson and Dumas Malone, *et al.*, eds., *Dictionary of American Biography* (New York: Scribner's, 1943–), vol. 8, pp. 587–88; Dorothy Hitzka, "Farm Colonies of the Salvation Army and in particular The Ft. Herrick Colony, Mentor, Ohio" (Cleveland: The Salvation Army Divisional Headquarters, March, 1976), typescript, pp. 12–13, SAA.

CHAPTER FOUR: FORT ROMIE, CALIFORNIA

1. From Brigadier John C. Addie, "A Good Social Song" (tune: "There'll Be a Hot Time in the Old Town Tonight"), *The War Cry* (SF), April 30, 1898.

2. *Harbor Lights* 1 (January, 1898):27.

3. San Francisco *Bulletin*, September 16, 1897; Oakland *Times*, October 6, 1897; *Salinas Evening Democrat*, January 17, 1898.

4. Booth-Tucker, "Farm Colonies" (1), p. 985; *Salinas Evening Democrat*, December 29, 1897; George W. Shaw, *The California Sugar Industry*, Part 1, University of California Agricultural Experiment Station *Bulletin* No. 149 (Sacramento: State Printer, 1903), pp. 21, 39.

5. Fort Romie Real Estate Account, Colonization Department Cash Books, Finance Department Film File F132, SAA, cited hereafter as Colonization Cash Books, SAA; deed of October 3, 1899, between Charles Romie and Frederick de L. Booth-Tucker, Deeds Book 61, p. 54; deed of January 1, 1901, between Salvation Army and North American Trust Company, Mortgages Book 33, pp. 6—7, both books in Monterey County Courthouse, Salinas, California.

6. Oakland *Times*, October 6, 1897; *The War Cry* (SF), October 8 and 9, 1897.

7. *The War Cry* (SF), October 23 and 30, 1897; *The War Cry* (NY), December 4, 1897.

8. *The War Cry* (SF), October 9 and 16; November 13 and 27; December 4, 1897; *The War Cry* (NY), October 16, 1897; *All the World* 18 (October, 1897):462; *The Pacific Rural Press* 55 (March 26, 1898):195.

9. *Harbor Lights* 1 (February, 1898):52; *The War Cry* (SF), January 1 and 15, 1898; entries for January 1 and 4, 1898, Diary of John E. T. Milsaps, 3 (new series), Milsaps MSS.

10. Entries for January 5 and 6, 1898, Diary of John E. T. Milsaps 3 (new series), Milsaps MSS; *Salinas Evening Democrat*, January 5, 1898.

11 Entries for January 5 and 6, 1898, Diary of John E. T. Milsaps, 3 (new series), Milsaps MSS; *Salinas Evening Democrat*, January 5, 1898; *Salinas Daily Journal*, January 6, 1898; *The War Cry* (SF), December 11, 1897 and January 22, 1898.

12. *San Francisco Examiner*, January 6, 1898; clipping, Salinas *Index*, January 6, 1898, Milsaps Scrapbook 2; entry for March 7, 1898, Diary of John E. T. Milsaps, 3 (new series), Milsaps MSS; *The War Cry* (SF), March 19, 1898; *The War Cry* (NY), December 4, 1897; *The Pacific Rural Press* 55 (January 8; February 5; March 19 and 26, 1898):18, 83, 179, 195.

13. *The War Cry* (NY), April 16, 1898; *The War Cry* (SF), April 2, 1898; Frederick de L. Booth-Tucker, *A Review of the Salvation Army Land Colony in California* (/1903?/), p. /25/.

14. Undated agreement, blank copy, AS 26-2-16, SAA.

15. Quoted in *The Pacific Rural Press* 55 (February 12, 1898):99.

16. Recommendation form, blank and undated, Salvation Army in America File, SAA. Cited hereafter as SAIA, SAA.

17. Blank form for Fort Romie Colony, SAIA, SAA.

18. *Salinas Daily Journal*, March 22, 1898; *The War Cry* (SF), March 26; April 16; June 11; July 30, 1898; *Harbor Lights* 1 (July, 1898):228; *Salinas Evening Democrat*, January 12 and 14; April 15, 1898.

19. *Salinas Evening Democrat*, April 15 and June 11, 1898; *Salinas Daily Journal*, March 22, 1898; *The War Cry* (SF), March 26; April 2 and 16; June 28; July 30; August 6; November 5, 1898; Charles D. Marx, "Report on Irrigation Problems in the Salinas Valley," in Elwood Mead, *Report on Irrigation Investigations in California* (U.S. D.A. Office of Experiment Stations *Bulletin* No. 100, Washington: Government Printing Office, 1901), pp. 194, 202.

20. *The War Cry* (SF), July 30, 1898.

21. *The War Cry* (SF), April 16; July 30; August 6; November 5, 1898; *All the World* 19 (October, 1898):478; Salvation Army Colonization Board Minutes, August 25, 1898, AS-11, SAA.

22. Entry for April 5, 1898, Diary of John E. T. Milsaps, 3 (new series), Milsaps MSS; Salvation Army Colonization Board Minutes, August 12 and 25; September 1; November 25, 1898, SAA; Wisbey, *Soldiers Without Swords*, pp. 89, 157—58.

23. Salvation Army Colonization Board Minutes, August 12, 1898. SAA.

24. *Ibid.*

25. *Ibid.*, August 12 and 24; September 1, 1898; List of documents transferred to Sold Properties 1/28/1920, in Property Department Records on Romie, Ac. 82-76. Cited hereafter as PDR Romie, SAA.

26. *The War Cry* (SF), November 5, 1898.

27. San Francisco *Call*, cited in *The War Cry* (NY), January 14, 1899.

28. *The War Cry* (SF), July 14 and August 18, 1900; *The War Cry* (NY), September 1, 1900; *The War Cry* (London), October 20, 1900.

29. Marx, "Report on Irrigation Problems," p. 202; *The War Cry* (SF), July 7; August 11 and 25, 1900; *The War Cry* (NY), July 14, 1900.

30. Haggard, *The Poor and the Land*, p. 39.

31. *All the World* 25 (September, 1904):499 – 500; *The War Cry* (SF), June 25, 1898; *The War Cry* (NY), July 4, 1903.

32. Booth-Tucker, *A Review of the Salvation Army Land Colony in California*, p. /25/; Haggard, *The Poor and the Land*, pp. 39, 46.

33. Haggard, *The Poor and the Land*, pp. 39 – 40, 47; Wisbey, *Soldiers Without Swords*, p. 130.

34. U.S. Ms Census of Monterey County, California, 1900.

35. Haggard, *The Poor and the Land*, p. 47.

36. Haggard, *The Poor and the Land*, p. 40; Booth-Tucker, *A Review of the Salvation Army Land Colony in California*, p. /12/; *The War Cry* (NY), July 4, 1903.

37. Haggard, *The Poor and the Land*, pp. 55, 56 – 59, 60; U.S. Ms Census of Monterey County, California, 1900.

38. Haggard, *The Poor and the Land*, pp. 55, 56, 58, 60, 61, 66; Thomas Holland to Frederick Booth-Tucker, August 10, 1903; Nels Erikson to Booth-Tucker, August 13, 1903; Erikson to Holland, August 13, 1903, copy; Erikson to Madison J. H. Ferris, October 5, 1903, all in PDR Romie, SAA; deed of September 23, 1903, between Salvation Army and Mathias Mathiesen, Deeds Book 75, pp. 403-4, Monterey County Courthouse.

39. U.S. Ms Census of Lake County, Ohio, 1900; Haggard, *The Poor and the Land*, p. 61; *The War Cry* (NY), March 21, 1903.

40. Booth-Tucker testimony (October 3, 1905), *Minutes of Evidence Taken Before the Departmental Committee Appointed to Consider Mr. Rider Haggard's Report on Agricultural Settlements in British Colonies, With Appendices, Analysis, and Index*, 2 House of Commons Sessional Papers (1906), 76:33, cited hereafter as *Minutes of Evidence*; *The War Cry* (SF), November 5, 1898; Booth-Tucker, "Farm Colonies" (1), pp. 983, 986.

41. See Chapter 8, p. 95.

42. Erikson to Madison J.H. Ferris, September 15, 1902, copy, PDR Romie, SAA.

43. Ferris to Erikson, November 14 and December 31, 1902, copies, PDR Romie, SAA; Fort Romie Cash Book, Finance Department Bound Ledgers, microfilm, pp. 18, 36, 41. Cited hereafter as Romie Cash Book, SAA.

44. Deed of November 27, 1899, between Charles T. Romie and Frederick Booth-Tucker, copy; Ferris to Erikson, April 16 and 18, 1902, copies; Holland to Ferris, April 8, 1903; Edward J. Higgins to Ferris, April 13, 1903, copy; Ferris to Higgins, April 15, 1903, all in PDR Romie, SAA.

45. Nels A. Erikson Statement (June, 1934), typescript; resolution of September 10, 1903, Romie Water Company; Holland to Ferris, March 24, 1903; Erikson to Holland, August 20, 1903, all in PDR Romie, SAA.

46. The plant took its water from the Salinas River and its tributary, Arroyo Seco Creek. When the company was formed, the system included an 80-horsepower Eclipse engine, an 80-horsepower return-flue boiler, a 16-inch Byron and Jackson closed runner centrifugal pump, suction and discharge pipe and much miscellaneous equipment, including boiler house, smokestack, complete oil-burning outfit, 900-foot main flume, 160-foot irrigation flume, 3.5 miles of main ditches, gates, and right-of way. Deed of conveyance, undated. Salvation Army to "Fort Romie Water Company," draft, in PDR Romie, SAA.

47. Garth V. Lacey to The Salvation Army, June 8 and 20, 1934, PDR Romie, SAA.

48. Entry for May 8, 1903, Diary of Frederick Booth-Tucker, microfilm, SAA; Booth-Tucker, *A Review of the Salvation Army Land Colony in California*, pp. /18–20/; *The War Cry* (NY), March 21 and July 4, 1903.

49. *The War Cry* (NY), October 29, 1904; Erikson to Ferris, October 16, 1903, PDR Romie, SAA. Developed in the 1840s by tradesmen at Rochdale in England, the idea of the cash cooperative store was that it worked in the economic interest of the customers, not the proprietors. Normally the Rochdale plan charged the backers a small entrance fee and sold them stock, often at ten percent down, the balance payable from future dividends. Part of the profit went into a reserve fund; the rest went to customers as dividends proportional to their purchases. Grant, *Self-Help in the 1890s Depression*, pp. 63–64.

50. *The War Cry* (NY), October 29, 1904; Haggard, *The Poor and the Land*, p. 43; *General Announcement, Fort Romie Rochdale Company* (Soledad, May 19, 1904); Erikson to Holland, May 9, 1904; Holland to Edward J. Higgins, May 17 and 26, 1904, all in PDR Romie, SAA; Romie Cash Book, pp. 88, 89, 95, 120, 123, 128, SAS.

51. Holland to Gustav Reinhardsen, September 16, 1902; J. D. McDougall to The Salvation Army, September 10, 1904; Ferris to Erikson, September 16, 1904, copy; Erikson to Ferris, September 27, 1904; F. S. Clark to The Salvation Army, September 7, 1906, all in PDR Romie, SAA.

52. *The War Cry* (NY), April 23 and October 29, 1904; *The War Cry* (London), April 15, 1905.

53. Ferris to Erikson, September 4, 1903, copy, PDR Romie, SAA.

54. The rental fee for the first year was to be $700; the second year $1,000. Purchase could be made with $5,000 down and a note for another $8,000. Erikson to Ferris, November 3, 1903, PDR Romie, SAA.

55. Erikson to Ferris, August 25, 1905; Ferris to Erikson, January 10, 1906, copy, PDR Romie, SAA. A list of documents transferred to Sold Properties, January 28, 1920, indicates "cancelled" was marked on the 1903 lease. PDR Romie, SAA.

56. Erikson to Ferris, November 11, 1903, PDR Romie, SAA.

57. Ferris to Erikson, November 24, 1903, copy; Erikson to Ferris, November 11, 1903, both in PDR Romie, SAA.

58. Holland to Ferris, March 11, 1904; Ferris to Holland, March 24, 1904, copy; Holland to Ferris, October 12, 1904; copy of agreement proposed in 1903 between The Salvation Army and colonist at Fort Romie (undated, blank), all in PDR Romie, SAA.

59. "One day word came that a 'poet feller' Rudyard Kipling was on his way to Fort Romie," sent by the British to inspect the colony. Kipling was enchanted with the place. "He stayed a week and was feasted off the land," all the while telling the colonists what a great enterprise they were engaged in. Fisher, *The Salinas*, p. 260.

60. See Chapter 9, pp. 105–9.

61. Haggard, *The Poor and the Land*, pp. 56–61, 62, 64–65; The Salvation Army, *Annual Statements 1905* (New York: Salvation Army, 1905).

62. *The War Cry* (NY), February 19, 1906. A notation in the cash book indicates that Romig took over from Erikson on January 26, 1906. Romie Cash Book, SAA. p. 161.

63. Erikson to Ferris, November 11, 1905, PDR Romie, SAA.

64. Fort Romie Loan Account, Colonization Cash Books, SAA. Figures are as of September 30, except for 1907, which is as September 28.

CHAPTER FIVE: FORT AMITY, COLORADO

1. Untitled (tune:"Ring the Bell, Watchman"), *The War Cry* (NY), September 3, 1904. Sketchy information on Fort Amity may be found in Dorothy Roberts, "Fort Amity, the Salvation Army Colony in Colorado," *The Colorado Magazine* 17 (September,

1940): 168–74. Marie Antalek, "The Amity Colony," M.A. Thesis, Kansas State Teachers College of Emporia, 1968, is a workmanlike job, but was written before the opening of official records by the Salvation Army Archives and Research Center.

2. *The War Cry* (NY), July 17, 1899; Helen Fletcher Collins, "The Beginning of Holly," *The Colorado Magazine* 27 (January, 1951):50.

3. *The War Cry* (NY), July 17, 1899; Dena S. Markoff, "A Bittersweet Saga: The Arkansas Valley Beet Sugar Industry, 1900–1979," *The Colorado Magazine* 56 (Summer/Fall, 1979):168.

4. Haggard, *The Poor and the Land*, pp. 67, 74; *Rocky Mountain News*, January 1, 1899; Land Contract of September 28, 1897, William N. Coler, Jr. to Frederick Booth-Tucker, No. 3314, Guaranty Abstract Company, Lamar, Colorado; warranty deed of July 26, 1901, Amity Land Company to Frederick de L. Booth-Tucker, Warranty Deed Book 48, pp. 12–13, Prowers County Courthouse, Lamar, Colorado. Warranty deeds and Warranty Deed Books are cited hereafter as deeds and Deed Books.

5. Booth-Tucker to Richard Holz, June 3, 1898, Holz MSS, SAA; *New York Herald*, December 25, 1898; *The War Cry* (NY), January 21, 1899; *Rocky Mountain News*, January 1, 1899; J. D. Whelpley, "Salvation Army Colonies," *Harper's Weekly* 45 (September, 1901):902; Albert Shaw, "A Successful Farm Colony in the Irrigation Country," *The American Monthly Review of Reviews* 26 (November, 1902):562; *All the World* 19 (June, 1898):251–52; 21 (November, 1900):624–25.

6. "Making Successful Farmers of City Failures," *World's Work* 6 (September, 1903): 3929–30; *New York Herald*, December 25, 1898. Names of the first groups of settlers and the places whence their fares were paid to Holly are found in undated Cash Book, in Farm Colonies: MS 5-1-1, SAA. Cited hereafter as Amity Cash Book, SAA.

7. Amity Cash Book, SAA.

8. *The War Cry* (NY), June 11, 1898.

9. At least three who were originally scheduled were cancelled out. Amity Cash Book, SAA. The Denver *Rocky Mountain News* believed that there were eighteen or nineteen families, while the Lamar editor put the figure at "about thirty." *Rocky Mountain News*, January 1, 1899; *Lamar Register*, April 23, 1898.

10. Amity Cash Book, SAA; *Harbor Lights* 1 (June, 1898):172; Mrs. Emielice Baldwin to Julia Stokes, no date, 1936, isolated letter, Colorado Historical Society, Denver.

11. *The War Cry* (NY), June 11, 1898; June 24, 1899; *Harbor Lights* 1 (June, 1898):173; *Rocky Mountain News*, January 1, 1899; Amity Cash Book, SAA.

12. *The War Cry* (NY), November 11, 1899; Emielice Baldwin to Julia Stokes, no date, 1936, Colorado Historical Society; *Rocky Mountain News*, January 1, 1899.

13. *The War Cry* (NY), June 11, 1898.

14. *The War Cry* (London), June 25, 1898; *The War Cry* (NY), June 11, 1898 and November 11, 1899; *Harbor Lights* 1 (June, 1898):172; *Holly Chieftain*, April 22, 1898; *The Syracuse Journal*, July 15, 1898; A. J. Davy Interview (February 6, 1934), Prowers County Interviews, Colorado Historical Society, Denver.

15. *Harbor Lights* 1 (June, 1898):172; *The War Cry* (NY), June 11 1898 and November 11, 1899; Haggard, *The Poor and the Land*, pp. 76, 85; *Rocky Mountain News*, January 1, 1899; *Holly Chieftain*, April 22 and October 14, 1898.

16. *Harbor Lights* 1 (June, 1898):172; *Holly Chieftain*, April 22 and 29, 1898; A. J. Davy Interview (February 6, 1934).

17. *Holly Chieftain*, April 29 and June 10, 1898; *The War Cry* (NY), June 11, 1898; June 24 and November 11, 1899.

18. *Holly Chieftain*, May 27 and August 19, 1898; *The War Cry* (SF), July 16, 1898.

19. *New York Herald*, December 25, 1898.

20. *Rocky Mountain News*, January 1, 1899; *Holly Chieftain*, April 29, 1898.

21. *Holly Chieftain*, April 22, 1898; *Rocky Mountain News*, January 1, 1899.

22. *Holly Chieftain*, April 22, 1898; *Rocky Mountain News*, January 1, 1899.

23. Haggard, *The Poor and the Land*, p. 76; *New York Herald*, December 25, 1898.

24. For example, see contract of December 21, 1900, between The Salvation Army and George H. Thomas, Miscellaneous Records Book 59, pp. 98–99, Prowers County Courthouse.

25. *Holly Chieftain*, April 22, 1898; *The War Cry* (NY), June 11, 1898; Booth-Tucker Memorandum of August 12, 1898, *re* conversation with W. Wiley on Fort Amity, included with Colonization Board Minutes, August 25, 1898, SAA.

26. *Holly Chieftain*, January 20, 1899; *New York Herald*, December 25, 1898; Denver *Times*, March 12, 1899; A. J. Davy Interview (February 6, 1934); Philo K. Blinn, "Development of the Rockyford Cantaloupe Industry," Agricultural Experiment Station of the Colorado Agricultural College *Bulletin* No. 108 (Fort Collins: March, 1906), pp. 6–8, 11.

27. *Holly Chieftain*, October 28, 1898 and January 20, 1899; Denver *Times*, March 12, 1899.

28. *New York Herald*, December 25, 1898.

29. Denver *Times*, March 12, 1899.

30. *The War Cry* (SF), September 17, 1898.

31. Colonization Board Minutes, August 25, 1898, SAA.

32. Land contract of October 14, 1899, between the Amity Land Company and the Salvation Army, Guaranty Abstract Company, Lamar; warranty deeds of January 1, February 9 and April 1, 1907, between the Arkansas Valley Sugar Beet and Irrigation Land Company and the Salvation Army, all in Warranty Deeds Book 67, pp. 312, 313, 314, Prowers County Courthouse; deeds of Trust of January 1, February 9 and April 1, 1907, between the Arkansas Valley Sugar Beet and Irrigated Land Company and the Salvation Army, all in Deed of Trust Book 53, pp. 437, 438, 439. After these transactions to the Salvation Army, the Amity Land Company transferred much of its land and water rights to the A.V.S.B. & I.L. Co., which ultimately completed the business with the Army.

33. *New York Herald*, cited in *The War Cry* (NY), January 21 and June 17, 1899; February 24, 1900; *Holly Chieftain*, April 27 and August 31, 1900.

34. Frederick Booth-Tucker, *What Others Think of the Salvation Army Colony at Amity, Prowers County, Colorado* (no place, no publisher, 1904), p. 5; Denver *Republican*, April 23, 1903; Haggard, *The Poor and the Land*, p. 68.

35. *Lamar Register*, February 22, 1899; *The War Cry* (NY), June 17, 1899.

36. Finance Council Minutes, October 17, 1899; March 16 and April 18, 1900, SAA; *All the World* 21 (November, 1900): 625; *Holly Chieftain*, June 23, 1899; March 9, 16, and 23; April 27, 1900; February 12, 1904; June 30, 1905. For an explanation of the Finance Council, see Chapter 7, pp. 87–88.

37. Finance Council Minutes, April 2 and June 8, 1900; May 16, 1902, SAA; *Holly Chieftain*, May 2, 1902.

38. Haggard, *The Poor and the Land*, pp. 84, 87, 96; *Pueblo Chieftain*, December 7, 1947.

39. Haggard, *The Poor and the Land*, p. 100; *Holly Chieftain*, June 7 and December 6, 1907.

40. Booth-Tucker Memorandum of August 12, 1898, *re* conversation with W. Wiley on Fort Amity, included with Colonization Board Minutes, August 25, 1898, SAA; Booth-Tucker to Herbert Booth, July 10, 1899, copy, "confidential," National Commander Collection, SAA.

41. Haggard, *The Poor and the Land*, pp. 92–93; *Holly Chieftain*, February 28, 1902.

42. Haggard, *The Poor and the Land*, pp. 83–96; Finance Council Minutes, January 19, May 22 and June 21, 1900; April 3, 1901; April 2, 1908, SAA; *Holly Chieftain*, February 23 and September 7, 1900; February 28 and April 18, 1902.

43. Haggard, *The Poor and the Land*, pp. 84, 86, 87, 96; *Holly Chieftain*, June 21, 1901; March 14 and April 4, 1902; *The War Cry* (SF), September 22, 1900.

44. *Holly Chieftain*, August 10 and 31; September 14; November 15, 1900; January 12 and May 24, 1901; February 28 and March 21, 1902; *The War Cry* (NY), October 18, 1901.

45. Holland to Ferris, September 7, 1903, Property Department, Legal Secretary Correspondence, SAA. Cited hereafter as LSC, SAA.

46. *Chicago Record-Herald*, November 24, 1904; *Progress of the Beet-Sugar Industry in the United States in 1904* (U.S. D.A. *Report* No. 80, Washington: Government Printing Office, 1905), p. 48; Markoff, "A Bittersweet Saga," pp. 166−68.

47. Markoff, "A Bittersweet Saga," 168; *Lamar Register*, September 4, 1901; *Holly Chieftain*, May 12, 1905.

48. *Holly Chieftain*, May 24, June 21 and November 29, 1901; April 4, May 16 and 23, 1902; June 3, 1904; August 3, 1906; Shaw, "A Successful Farm Colony," 564.

49. *The War Cry* (NY), September 1, 1900; *Holly Chieftain*, May 30, June 13 and October 17, 1902; Nels Erikson to Ferris, August 15, 1907, Property Department Correspondence, Amity file, 22-8-19, SAA. Cited hereafter as Amity Correspondence, SAA.

50. *Holly Chieftain*, May 30, October 2 and 31, 1902; Ferris to Brigadier T. W. Scott, July 3, 1902, copy, LSC, SAA.

51. "How About the Depot?" from *Amity Optimist*, quoted in *The War Cry* (NY), September 3, 1904.

52. Booth-Tucker to Herbert Booth, July 10, 1899, copy, "confidential," National Commander Collection, SAA.

53. Booth-Tucker to Richard Holz, July 22, 1898, Holz MSS, SAA.

54. *Holly Chieftain*, May 2, 1902; June 22, 1903; July 7 and 14, 1905.

55. *Holly Chieftain*, June 10 and October 28, 1898; February 3, 1899; Denver *Times*, March 12, 1899; *The War Cry* (NY), November 18, 1898.

56. *Holly Chieftain*, May 5, 1899; June 21 and 28, 1901; Denver *Times*, March 12, 1899; *The War Cry* (SF), August 11 and 25, September 22, 1900; *The War Cry* (NY), October 22, 1904; *All the World* 25 (November, 1900):625.

57. *The War Cry* (NY), September 1, 1900; *Holly Chieftain*, September 7, 1900; September 20, 1901.

58. *Holly Chieftain*, September 27, 1901.

59. Antalek, "The Amity Colony," p. 47. Antalek suggests that this implies managerial problems; or it may indicate that Holland was something of a trouble-shooter. Certainly, he circulated among Forts Amity, Romie, and Herrick with some frequency.

60. *Holly Chieftain*, August 4, 1899; *The War Cry* (NY), June 17, 1899; *Rocky Mountain News*, July 27, 1902; Holland to Ferris, March 25, 1903; Holland to Finance Council, October 12, 1905; Holland to Booth-Tucker, August 18, 1903; Ferris to Holland, September 3, 1903, copy, all in LSC, SAA.

61. *Holly Chieftain*, May 4, 1900; *The War Cry* (NY), May 5, July 4 and August 11, 1900.

62. *Holly Chieftain*, May 4, 1900; March 1 and May 17, 1901; April 11, 1902; Haggard, *The Poor and the Land*, pp. 81−82; Wisbey, *Soldiers without Swords*, pp. 70−71; Erikson to Holland, May 11, 1906, Amity Correspondence, SAA.

63. "Where to Take Your Troubles," from the *Amity Optimist*, quoted in *The War Cry* (NY), September 3, 1904.

64. Booth-Tucker to Herbert Booth, February 2, 1902, copy, National Commander Collection, SAA; *Chicago Tribune*, July 20,1902; *Holly Chieftain*, August 31, 1900; Finance Council Minutes, May 22 and June 8, 1900, SAA; Haggard, *The Poor and the Land*, pp. 94−95, 112.

65. Haggard, *The Poor and the Land*, p. 98; *Holly Chieftain*, March 1 and June 28, 1901; February 14, 1902.

66. Haggard, *The Poor and the Land*, p. 97; *Holly Chieftain*, February 14, May 23 and October 3, 1902; May 1 and June 19, 1908; Finance Council Minutes, January 29, 1903; James H. Childs Account, Colonization Cash Books, SAA; deed of trust of May 22, 1903, J. H. Childs to the Salvation Army, Trust Deed Record Book 33, p. 349; deed of trust of January 11, 1904, J. H. Childs to the Salvation Army, Trust Deed Record Book 37, p. 425; release of Deed of Trust of April 1, 1908, the Salvation Army to James H. Childs, Release Record Book 50, p. 271. All deeds of trust and releases in Prowers County Courthouse.

67. Haggard, *The Poor and the Land*, pp. 85—86, 88—89; *Holly Chieftain*, March 4 and 28, April 4, July 18, August 22 & October 3, 1902; July 5 and 28, 1905.

68. Haggard, *The Poor and the Land*, pp. 83, 98—99; *Holly Chieftain*, October 25, 1901; February 28, April 4 and 18, May 16, June 6, September 12 and 26, 1902.

69. Haggard, *The Poor and the Land*, p. 70; A. J. Davy Interview (February 6, 1934); Glenn Shirley, *Henry Starr: Last of the Real Badmen* (New York: David McKay Co., 1965), p. 158; Ralph C. Taylor, *Colorado South of the Border* (Denver: Sage Books, 1963), p. 273; Booth-Tucker, "Farm Colonies" (1), p. 985; Booth-Tucker, *What Others Think*, p. 28.

70. Finance Council Minutes, March 25, June 4, September 11, December 4, 1902; January 29, 1903; March 14 and November 15, 1907, SAA; *Holly Chieftain*, March 4 and October 3, 1902.

71. Shaw, "A Successful Farm Colony," p. 564; *The War Cry* (NY), May 9, 1903.

72. *Holly Chieftain*, April 21 and 28, 1899; February 15, March 1 and May 25, 1901; March 4, 1902; April 17, 1903.

73. Joseph H. Hargreaves Interview (January 30, 1934), Prowers County Interviews, Colorado Historical Society, Denver; *The War Cry* (NY), May 10, 1902; September 3, 1904; *Holly Chieftain*, February 28, March 4, October 3, and November 14, 1902; September 16, 1903; March 25, June 12 and 23, 1905; August 2, 1907; Booth-Tucker, *What Others Think*, p. 25.

74. *The War Cry* (SF), June 16, 1898. By mid-October, Sadie Gunnerson was in charge of about twenty students. *Holly Chieftain*, October 14, 1898. Another source says that A. G. Glase was the first teacher. Antalek, "The Amity Colony," p. 49. Late in April 1900, the local papers noted that "Miss Gunnison" was spending her last day in the colony as teacher. *Holly Chieftain*, April 27, 1900.

75. *Holly Chieftain*, November 11, 1898; May 5, 1899; Denver *Times*, March 2, 1899; Booth-Tucker to Herbert Booth, July 10, 1899, copy, "confidential," National Commander Collection, SAA.

76. *Holly Chieftain*, October 25, 1901; April 17, 1903; *The War Cry* (NY), May 9, 1903; Haggard, *The Poor and the Land*, p. 114; Booth-Tucker, "Farm Colonies" (1), p. 985.

77. *Rocky Mountain News*, July 27, 1902; *New York Herald*, December 25, 1898; *The War Cry* (NY), January 21, 1899; *Holly Chieftain*, April 22, 1898.

78. *All the World* 21 (November, 1900):626.

79. Booth-Tucker to Herbert Booth, February 2, 1902, copy, National Commander Collection, SAA.

80. *Holly Chieftain*, October 14, 1898; March 10, 1899.

81. *Holly Chieftain*, April 7 and 21, 1899; *The War Cry* (NY), March 3, 1899.

82. *The War Cry* (NY), February 24, 1900; *The War Cry* (SF), August 25, 1900.

83. *Holly Chieftain*, October 28, 1898; January 6, March 10, and December 29, 1899; *The War Cry* (NY), November 18, 1898; Wisbey, *Soldiers Without Swords*, p. 73.

84. Wisbey, *Soldiers Without Swords*, p. 137; *The War Cry* (SF), July 29, 1899; *The War Cry* (NY), May 11, 1901; October 24 and November 14, 1903; *Holly Chieftain*, April 27, 1900; *All the World* 25 (September, 1904):497.

85. *The War Cry* (NY), May 9, 1903; October 22, 1904; *Holly Chieftain*, April 17, 1903; entries for April 18 and 19, Diary of Frederick Booth-Tucker, SAA; *All the World* 25 (December, 1904):681.

86. *The War Cry* (NY), November 24 and December 8, 1900.

87. *The War Cry* (NY), May 11 and October 19, 1901; Denver *Times*, March 16, 1902; *La Junta Tribune*, July 28, 1945; Booth-Tucker, *What Others Think*, pp. 18, 26; Joseph H. Hargreaves Interview (January 30, 1934).

88. *New York Times*, September 9, 1901; *Holly Chieftain*, September 14, 1900; June 21 and 28; August 11, 1901; May 27, 1904; *La Junta Tribune*, July 28, 1945; *The War Cry* (NY), October 19, 1901; Booth-Tucker, *What Others Think*, pp. 19—20, 27; Joseph H. Hargreaves Interview (January 30, 1934); Denver *Republican*, December 4, 1903.

89. Joseph H. Hargreaves Interview (January 30, 1943): A. J. Davy Interview (February 6, 1934). Wisbey says the children were moved to Spring Valley, New York;

McKinley says they returned to New Jersey. Wisbey, *Soldiers Without Swords*, p. 133; McKinley, *Marching to Glory*, p. 91.

90. *Holly Chieftain*, July 27, 1900; Booth-Tucker interview (Kansas City, August 31, 1901), quoted in *Lamar Register*, September 4, 1901; *The War Cry* (NY), August 11, 1901.

91. *The War Cry* (NY), August 12, 1905; *Holly Chieftain*, June 23, 1905; August 10, 1906; September 6 and 13, 1907; Antalek, "The Amity Colony," pp. 55 — 56; A. J. Davy Interview (February 6, 1934); Land and Land Improvement Account, Colonization Cash Books, SAA.

92. *Denver Republican*, April 23, 1903; *Holly Chieftain*, July 27, 1900; *The War Cry* (NY), October 22, 1898; Booth-Tucker, "Farm Colonies" (1), pp. 987 — 88.

93. Haggard, *The Poor and the Land*, pp. 88, 90 — 91, 93 — 94, 95, 96; Joseph H. Hargreaves Interview (January 30, 1934); A. J. Davy Interview (February 6, 1934); *The War Cry* (NY), June 11, 1898; *Holly Chieftain*, October 28, 1898; June 21, 1901; June 23, 1905.

94. For references to other Corps officers who came to Amity for reasons of health, see *Holly Chieftain*, October 14, 1898; April 21, 1899; September 14, 1900; June 27, 1902; June 23, 1905; Haggard, *The Poor and the Land*, pp. 92 — 93, 93 — 94.

95. Haggard, *The Poor and the Land*, pp. 85, 86 — 87, 88 — 89, 90, 91 — 92, 94 — 95, 100.

96. *Ibid.*, pp. 83 — 84, 85 — 86, 89, 92, 98 — 99; *Denver Times*, March 12, 1899.

97. Haggard, *The Poor and the Land*, pp. 84 — 85, 93, 94, 95, 96, 100.

98. *Ibid.*, pp. 84, 90 — 91.

99. *The War Cry* (NY), March 29, 1902.

100. *Holly Chieftain*, September 9, 1898; Holland to Board of Trustees of the Salvation Army, April 2, 1906, copy, LSC, SAA. Over a period of time, irrigation water percolating through the soil failed to leach the salts out and eventually left a saline concentration damaging to plant growth. McKinley is in error when he attributes the salt problem to the backing up of the Arkansas River. McKinley, *Marching to Glory*, p. 91. To be sure, the river did once inundate Amity and many of the colony lands in flood season, but this was in 1908, well after the saline damage had been done. *Holly Chieftain*, October 23, 1908.

101. Holland to the Board of Trustees of the Salvation Army, April 2, 1906, copy, LSC, SAA; *Holly Chieftain*, December 2, 1904; July 7, 1905; January 1, 1906.

102. Holland to the Board of Trustees of the Salvation Army, April 2, 1906, copy, LSC, SAA.

103. Minutes of Special Meeting of the Board of Trustees of the Salvation Army, March 23 and 24, 1906, draft, LSC, SAA.

104. Lieutenant Colonel Hicks to Holland, March 30, 1906, copy; Holland to the Board of Trustees of the Salvation Army, April 2, 1906, copy, both in LSC, SAA.

105. Finance Council Minutes, July 5, 1906, SAA.

106. *Holly Chieftain*, May 18, 1906 and March 1, 1907; Finance Council Minutes, February 8, 1907, SAA.

107. Finance Council Minutes, February 8, 1907, SAA.

108. Finance Council Minutes, February 21, March 14, April 4, November 15, and December 5, 1907; March 12 and April 2, 1908, SAA.

109. Finance Council Minutes, October 6, 1904; September 8, 1905; April 25 and May 23, 1907, SAA.

110. James H. Durand to Ferris, March 8, 1905; Holland to Ferris, July 1, 1905, LSC, SAA.

111. Ferris to Holland, July 21, 1905, LSC, SAA.

112. Roberts, "Fort Amity," pp. 173 — 74.

113. *Holly Chieftain*, April 2, 1909.

114. Deed of May 14, 1909, between the Salvation Army and J. S. McMurtry, Deed Book 70, p. 577; deed of March 5, 1909, between the Salvation Army and Joseph S. McMurtry and John G. Christopher, Miscellaneous Record Book 82, pp. 217 — 22;

deed of September 20, 1912, between the Salvation Army and J. S. McMurtry, Deeds Book 87, p. 129, all in Prowers County Courthouse; McMurtry and Christopher Account, Colonization Cash Books; Holland to Ferris, March 2, 1908, William S. Barker to Ferris, June 29 and July 26, 1909; Holland to William Peart, June 1, 1909, letters all in Amity Correspondence, SAA.

115. See Chapter 8, pp. 97–99.

116. Joseph H. Hargreaves Interview (January 30, 1934).

CHAPTER SIX: FORT HERRICK, OHIO

1. Madison J. H. Ferris to Richard Holz, May 31, 1898, copy, Fort Herrick Files, SAA.

2. *D. A. B.*, vol. 8, pp. 587–88; Myron T. Herrick to Booth-Tucker, November 1, 1904, Booth-Tucker Farewell Correspondence, MS 16-1–2, SAA; *New York Times*, February 22, 1904.

3. *The War Cry* (NY), September 17, 1898; Fort Herrick Real Estate Account, Colonization Cash Books, SAA.

4. William M. Gale to Richard Holz, May 10, 1898, Holz MSS, SAA; Ferris to Holz, June 1, 1898, copy, Fort Herrick Files, SAA; Booth-Tucker, "Farm Colonies" (1), p. 985.

5. Ferris to Holz, May 31, 1898, copy, Fort Herrick Files, SAA.

6. U.S. Ms Census of Lake County, Ohio, 1900; *The War Cry* (SF), July 9, 1898; Holz to Edward J. Higgins, June 22, 1898, copy; Booth-Tucker to Holz, January 18, 1899, copy, "personal"; Higgins to Holz, June 15, 1898, copy, all in Fort Herrick Files, SAA.

7. *The War Cry* (SF), July 9, 1898; Colonization Council Minutes, June 30, 1898, *The War Cry* (SF), July 9, 1898; *The War Cry* (NY), September 17, 1898.

8. *The War Cry* (NY), September 3 and 17, 1898; Hitzka, "Farm Colonies," p. 16.

9. *The War Cry* (SF), July 9, 1898; Fort Herrick agreement, blank undated copy, LSC, SAA.

10. *New York Herald*, December 25, 1898; Hitzka, "Farm Colonies," pp. 20-23. Early records indicate that there were two Harringtons among the colonists—W. Harrington and Burt Harrington. Finance Ledger for Fort Herrick Colony, June 1898–October 1901, Farm Colonies: M 50-1-3, pp. 141, 147. Cited hereafter as Fort Herrick Ledger, SAA.

11. *New York Herald*, December 25, 1898; Colonization Council Minutes, August 11 and 25, 1898, in Fort Herrick Files, SAA.

12. Richard Holz to Booth-Tucker, March 8, 1899, "personal," Fort Herrick Files, SAA.

13. *Ibid*.

14. *Ibid*.

15. Booth Tucker to Holz, July 22, 1898, copy, Fort Herrick Files, SAA.

16. Colonization Council Minutes, July 28, August 11 and October 26, 1898, all in Fort Herrick Files, SAA.

17. Colonization Council Minutes, October 26 and November 25, 1898, Fort Herrick Files, SAA.

18. Colonization Council Minutes, August 11, September 1 and December 1, 1898, Fort Herrick Files, SAA.

19. Colonization Council Minutes, July 7 and 14, 1898, Fort Herrick Files, SAA.

20. Fort Herrick Ledger, pp. 139, 140, 141, 142, SAA.

21. Fort Herrick Ledger, pp. 52, 131, 133, 134, SAA; Financial Council Minutes, July 25, 1901, SAA. Apparently the name of the Colonization Council was changed to the Financial Council.

22. Finance Council Minutes, October 1, 1901 and December 4, 1902, SAA.

23. *The War Cry* (NY), September 6, 1902; Fort Herrick Ledger, p. 157, SAA; Finance Council Minutes, April 13 and 25, September 11, 1902; March 10, 1903, SAA.

24. Joseph R. McFee to Ferris, October 1, 1902; Ferris to Holland, November 5, 1902, copy, both in LSC, SAA.
25. Finance Council Minutes, January 29, 1903; Ferris to Holland, September 8, 1903, copy, LSC, SAA.
26. *The War Cry* (NY), February 13, May 14 and October 29, 1904.
27. Booth-Tucker to Holz, January 18, 1899, copy, Fort Herrick Files, SAA; Fort Herrick Real Estate Account, Colonization Cash Books, SAA; Haggard, *The Poor and the Land*, p. 8; Booth-Tucker, "Farm Colonies" (1), pp. 1000–1001.
28. U.S. Ms Census of Lake County, Ohio, 1900; Haggard, *The Poor and the Land*, pp. 61, 90–91, 115, 120.
29. Fort Herrick Loan Account, Colonization Cash Books, SAA; "Brief compiled for London Conference, 1912"; Colonel D. Waldron to Richard E. Holz, August 12, 1974, copy, both the last two items are in Fort Herrick Files, SAA.

CHAPTER SEVEN:
THE DOLLARS AND CENTS OF COLONIZATION

1. From Brigadier Pebbles, "Colonization Song," *The War Cry* (NY), November 5, 1904.
2. *The War Cry* (SF), September 10, 1898.
3. Advertisement, "Grand Anniversary Rally," SAA; Booth-Tucker to A. W. Krech, December 15, 1898, copy, "personal," SAA.
4. *New York Times*, February 22, 1904; *All the World* 25 (April, 1904) :210; *The Salvation Army in the United States, Balance Sheets for the Year 1902* (New York: The Salvation Army, 1902), p. 12.
5. Finance Council Minutes, January 19, 1900; September 27, 1906; May 2 and 16, 1907, SAA; *The War Cry* (NY), July 4, 1903.
6. Arthur Desmond Shaw to Isaac Ellwood, June 20, 1902, Isaac Ellwood MSS, Box 65, University of Wyoming Library, Laramie; Booth-Tucker to Phoebe Hearst, no date: noted on back, "Ansd Nov 28/04," Phoebe Hearst MSS, Bancroft Library, University of California, Berkeley; *The War Cry* (NY), July 4, 1900.
7. *The War Cry* (NY), October 22, 1898.
8. *The War Cry* (SF), November 5, 1898.
9. Finance Council Minutes, May 10, 1900, SAA; Booth-Tucker, "Farm Colonies" (2), 759–60.
10. *The War Cry* (SF), July 21 and August 25, 1900; Charter, Salvation Army Colonization Association (June 1900), Ac. 84-62, SAA.
11. An Act to provide for the incorporation of the Salvation Army, April 28, 1899, *Laws of the State of New York, passed at the One Hundred and Twenty-Second Session of the Legislature, begun January Fourth, 1899, and ended April Twenty-Eighth, 1899, in the City of Albany* (Albany: Banks & Co., 1899), vol. 2, pp. 956–57.
12. Booth-Tucker to Bramwell Booth, December 22, 1898, copy, Incorporation File, SAA; Ferris to Platt Rogers, October 7, 1908, copy; Rogers to Ferris, October 13, 1908, Amity Correspondence, SAA.
13. *The War Cry* (NY), March 2 and May 31, 1901; Mortgage deed of January 1, 1901, between the Salvation Army and the North American Trust Company, Trust Deed Record Book 37, pp. 354–55, Monterey County Courthouse.
14. *The War Cry* (NY), February 28, 1903; list of bondholders as of September 30, 1904, Colonization Cash Books, SAA; *D.A.B.*, vol. 18, p. 622; *Who Was Who in America* (1897–1942) (Chicago: A. N. Marquis Co., 1943), vol. 1, pp. 381, 535, 1271.
15. Frederick de L. Booth-Tucker, *Prairie Homes For City Poor* (New York), pp. 3, 5, 7, 9, 11–12, 46; Booth-Tucker, "Farm Colonies" (1), pp. 986–87.
16. Colonization Loan Account, September 30, 1904, Colonization Cash Books, SAA; Colonization Department Cash Ledger, Film File 44, SAA. Cited hereafter as Colonization Ledger 44, SAA.

17. Colonization Loan Accounts, 1904–1914, Colonization Cash Books, SAA.

18. Booth-Tucker to Phoebe Hearst, no date: noted on back, "Ans^d Nov 28/04," Phoebe Hearst MSS.

19. See Chapter 5, pp. 61–62.

20. Income and Expense, year ending September 30, 1904, Central Colonization Department, The Salvation Army, *Annual Statement, 1904* (New York: The Salvation Army, 1904), no page numbers; Income and Expense, year ending September 30, 1905, Central Colonization Department, The Salvation Army, *Annual Statements, 1905* (New York: The Salvation Army, 1905), no page numbers; Exhibit "B", Income and Expenditures of the Colonization Department, year ending September 30, 1907, The Salvation Army, *Annual Statements, 1907* (New York: The Salvation Army, 1907), no page numbers; Profit and Loss, as of September 30, 1905, Colonization Cash Books, SAA; Minutes of Special Meeting of the Board of Trustees of the Salvation Army, March 23 and 24, 1906, draft, LSC, SAA.

21. The Salvation Army, *Annual Statements, 1904*, no page numbers; The Salvation Army, *Annual Statements, 1907*, no page numbers.

22. Act of April 28, 1899, *Laws of the State of New York* (1899), vol. 2, p. 956; see, for example, petitions approved August 25 and October 1, 1915; October 20 and 26, 1916; March 26, June 27, September 25 and November 19, 1917, all in Miscellaneous Records Book P, pp. 96–101, 108–12, 239–43, 343–47, 399–403, 429–32, 451–55, 458–62; also petitions approved July 3, October 20 and December 23, 1919, all in Miscellaneous Records Book R, pp. 322–28, 373–77, 400–04, all in Monterey County Courthouse.

23. Ferris to Holland, April 1, 1902, copy, LSC, SAA; Ferris to Erikson, November 7, 1903, copy; Erikson to Gustav Reinhardsen, February 17, 1905, copy, both in PDR Romie, SAA.

24. Ferris to Holland, June 30, 1905, copy; William S. Barker to Ferris, December 20, 1912, both in PDR Romie, SAA.

25. Holland to Erikson, July 8, 1903, copy; Ferris to Jacob U. Romig, July 23, 1907, copy; Romig to Ferris, August 10, 1907, copy, all in PDR Romie, SAA.

26. Holland to Ferris, November 12, 1901, LSC, SAA.

27. *Ibid.*; Haggard, *The Poor and the Land*, p. 93; U.S. Ms Census, Prowers County, Colorado, 1900.

28. Ferris to Holland, November 15, 1901, "confidential," copy, LSC, SAA.

29. Holland to Ferris, March 27, 1902; Ferris to Holland, March 31 and April 5, 1902, copies, LSC, SAA.

30. Ferris to Holland, May 1, 6 and 17, 1902, copies, LSC, SAA.

31. Holland to Ferris, July 31, 1902; Ferris to Holland, May 17 and August 4, 1902, copies, LSC, SAA.

32. Holland to Ferris, September 3 and 16, 1902; January 5, 1903; Ferris to Holland, September 26 and December 5, 1902; January 8, 1903, copies, LSC, SAA.

33. Ferris to Holland, January 27 and March 31, 1903, copies, LSC, SAA.

34. Release of Mortgage, May 6, 1902, North American Trust Company to the Salvation Army, Release Record Book 50, pp. 12–13, Prowers County Courthouse; Deed of March 28, 1903, Salvation Army to Ada M. Stimson, Abstracts Book 23, p. 383, Guaranty Abstract Company, Lamar.

35. Erikson to Holland, May 11, 1906, Amity Correspondence, SAA.

36. Release of Mortgage, May 24, 1917, Equitable Trust Company of New York to the Salvation Army, Release of Mortgages and Leases Book 11, pp. 114–16, Monterey County Courthouse; The Salvation Army, *Annual Statements, 1905*, no page numbers.

37. *The Salvation Army in the United States, Balance Sheets for the Year 1902*, p. 12; Colonization Cash Books, SAA.

38. *The War Cry* (NY), March 29, 1902.

39. Colonization Ledger 44, p. 3; Fort Romie Real Estate Account, Colonization Cash Books, SAA.

40. Colonization Ledger 44, p. 3, SAA.
41. *The Salvation Army in the United States, Balance Sheets for the Year 1902,* p. 13.
42. The Salvation Army, *Annual Statements, 1907*, no page numbers.
43. The more realistic 1910 book figures valued property and equipment at only $52,833.33; land and improvements accounted for only $17,408.88. The Salvation Army, *Balance Sheet and Statements of Account 1910* (New York: The Salvation Army, 1910).
44. *The Salvation Army Balance Sheet and Statements of Account 1920* (New York: The Salvation Army, 1920).
45. The Salvation Army, *Annual Statements, 1905.*
46. Haggard, *The Poor and the Land,* p. 39; Roberts, "Fort Amity," p. 174; Taylor, *Colorado South of the Border,* p. 273.
47. Mrs. Roland Wilkins, "General Booth and the Land," in *The Life of General Booth* (London & Edinburgh: T. Nelson & Sons, 1913?), pp. 214, 225, 238; *The War Cry* (SF), July 21, 1900.
48. Edward M. Higgins to Richard Holz, July 15, 1898, "personal," copy, Fort Herrick Files, SAA. Names of members have been gleaned from Minutes of the Council meetings.
49. Colonization Council Minutes, June 30, July 14, and 28, 1898, SAA.
50. See Chapter 6, p. 73.
51. Finance Council Minutes, July 1, 1899, SAA.
52. Finance Council Minutes, September 8, 1899; June 4, 1902, SAA. See Chapter 5, pp. 66–67.
53. Haggard, *The Poor and the Land*, p. 49; Profit and Loss Account, Colonization Cash Books, SAA.
54. See Finance Ledger from Amity Colony, Farm Colonies: MS 50-1-4, pp. 56, 80A, 105A, 171A, 171B, 220A, 221A, SAA. Cited hereafter as Amity Ledger, SAA; Romie Cash Book, SAA.
55. *Holly Chieftain,* February 3, 1899; Requisition, signed by Thomas Holland, April 30, 1902, LSC, SAA.
56. Finance Council Minutes, January 12, 1900; April 18 and June 13, 1901; July 14, 1902; January 29 and August 27, 1903, SAA.
57. *The Salvation Army Year Book for 1907* (London: Salvation Book Department, 1907), p. 65; Finance Council Minutes, June 1 and 22, August 4, September 8, 1899; April 18, 1900; May 23 and September 6, 1907, SAA; Amity Ledger, pp. 3, 56, 73, 261; Romie Cash Book, p. 7, SAA.
58. Finance Council Minutes, March 27, June 4, 1902; March 10, April 15, May 7 and June 26, 1903; January 15 and May 13, 1904, SAA; Ferris to Brigadier T. W. Scott, July 3, 1902, copy, LSC, SAA.
59. Finance Council Minutes, January 15 and May 26, 1904, SAA; Romie Cash Book, pp. 8, 45, 89, 91, 111, 157; Amity Ledger, pp. 3, 73, 81, 89, 107, 115, 119, 121, 153, 177, 217, 219, 261, SAA.
60. Ferris to Holland, November 15, 1901, copy, "confidential," LSC, SAA.
61. Ferris to Holland, May 6, 1902, copy, LSC, SAA.
62. Ferris to James H. Durand, December 5, 1904, copy, LSC, SAA.
63. Ferris to J. R. McKee, September 23, 1902, copy, LSC, SAA.
64. Ferris to Holland, March 19 and April 29, 1902, copies, LSC, SAA.
65. Haggard, *The Poor and the Land,* pp. 47–48.

CHAPTER EIGHT: THE COLONY BALANCE SHEET

1. Nels T. Erikson to Thomas Holland, May 11, 1906, Amity Correspondence, SAA.
2. *The War Cry* (NY), March 24, 1902. Two years earlier, the Commander had noted that the only person who had proved unfit had been relocated in Denver. *The War Cry*

(NY), January 21, 1899. A few months later, Thomas Holland said that Amity had lost but one colonist, who went with regret "only becasue a widowed mother in a distant part of the country had imperative need of his personal appearance." *The War Cry* (NY), June 17, 1899. Early in 1900, *The War Cry* stated that the only family to leave Amity so far had done so because of the death of its head. *The War Cry* (NY), February 24, 1900.

3. Haggard, *The Poor and the Land*, pp. 77–78.

4. Holland to E. D. Cox, October 12, 1905, copy; Holland to Finance Council, October 12, 1905; Ferris to Holland, December 13, 1905, copy, all in LSC, SAA.

5. *Holly Chieftain*, September 26, 1902.

6. James H. Childs Account, George H. Thomas Account, Colonization Cash Books, SAA; Assignment of Contract, November 19, 1909, George H. and Isabella Thomas to the Salvation Army, Abstracts Book N, p. 46, Guaranty Abstract Company, Lamar; Miscellaneous Records Book 72, p. 266, Prowers County Courthouse.

7. *Holly Chieftain*, February 16 and March 16, 1900; *The War Cry* (NY), March 3, 1900.

8. Holland to Charles Barkman, February 2, 1907, copy, Amity Correspondence, SAA.

9. James H. Durand to Ferris, March 7, 1905, Amity Correspondence, SAA.

10. Haggard, *The Poor and the Land*, p. 56; C. H. Hume Account; John and Frank Nelson Account, Colonization Cash Books, SAA; deed of September 23, 1913 between the Salvation Army and F. N. Nelson, *et al.*, Deeds Book 132, p. 27, Monterey County Courthouse.

12. A. C. Carle Account, Colonization Cash Books, SAA; deed of August 26, 1912 between the Salvation Army and Fred Evans, Deeds Book 127, p. 10, Monterey County Court House.

13. John Vrieling Account, Colonization Cash Books, SAA.

14. George H. Thomas Account, Colonization Cash Books, SAA; Assignment of Contract of November 19, 1909, George and Isabella Thomas to the Salvation Army, Abstracts Book N, p. 46, Guaranty Abstract Company, Lamar; Miscellaneous Records Book 72, p. 266, Prowers County Courthouse.

15. George Nicol Account, Colonization Cash Books, SAA; Haggard, *The Poor and the Land*, p. 85.

16. Haggard, *The Poor and the Land*, pp. 91–92; George Waidner Account, Colonization Cash Books, SAA.

17. Fort Amity Profit & Loss Account; Management Interest Account, Colonization Cash Books, SAA; Holland to Ferris, October 10, 1906, Amity Correspondence, SAA.

18. J. F. McAbee Account; Fort Amity Profit & Loss Account, Colonization Cash Books, SAA.

19. H. W. Manning Account; J. A. Ziegler Account, Colonization Cash Books, SAA.

20. James H. Childs Account; Greenard Estate Account, Colonization Cash Books, SAA; Haggard *The Poor and the Land*, pp. 99–100; Will of Mary R. Greenard, recorded July 22, 1908, certified copy, Abstracts Book K, P. 732, Guaranty Abstract Company, Lamar.

21. These figures are compiled from individual colonists' accounts and are not necessarily complete.

22. Haggard, *The Poor and the Land*, p. 56; U.S. Ms Census of Monterey County, California, 1900; Charles Johnson Account; C. M. Hodges Account, both in Colonization Cash Books, SAA; William S. Barker to Ferris, August 31, 1911 and February 7, 1912, both in PDR Romie, SAA.

23. Emil Baetschen Account, Colonization Cash Books, SAA; Barker to Ferris, June 13, 1910, PDR Romie, SAA; deed of January 6, 1916, between the Salvation Army and Catharine Baetschen, Deeds Book 142, p, 305; deed of October 21, 1916, between the Salvation Army and Ada Handley, Deeds Book 150, p. 272, both in Monterey County Courthouse.

24. U.S. Ms Census of Prowers County, Colorado, 1900; Management Interest Account, Colonization Cash Books, SAA.

25. Holland to Ferris, March 17, 1902, LSC, SAA.

26. Holland to Nels Erikson and Charles W. Bourne, June 4, 1902, copy, PDR Romie, SAA; *Holly Chieftain*, June 6 and 13, 1902.

27. *Holly Chieftain*, December 23, 1904.

28. Holland to E. D. Cox, October 12, 1905, copy; Holland to Finance Council, October 12, 1905; Ferris to Holland, December 13, 1905, copy, LSC, SAA.

29. Ferris to Holland, November 15, 1900, copy, "confidential"; March 31 and December 13, 1902, copies; Ferris to Henry Stillwell, December 3, 1901, copy, "personal," all in LCS, SAA.

30. Erik Erikson Account; George H. Thomas Account, Colonization Cash Books, SAA.

31. Holland to Ferris, September 9, 1902; Holland to S. A. Inman, February 11, 1902; Ferris to Holland, October 29, 1902, copy, all in LSC, SAA.

32. Holland to Ferris, January 3, 1902; Erikson to Ferris, July 26, 1902; Ferris to Erikson, September 4, 1902, copy; Erikson to Ferris, September 15, 1902, all in PDR Romie, SAA; Ferris to Holland, August 30, 1902, copy, LSC, SAA; deed of September 4, 1902, between the Salvation Army and Oscar Lindstrand, Deeds Book 71, p. 230; deed of June 20, 1913, between the Salvation Army and Oscar Lindstrand, Deeds Book 131, p. 116; deed of January 29, 1915, between the Salvation Army and Oscar Lindstrand, Deeds Book 138, pp. 183–84, Monterey County Court House.

33. See Chapter 4, p. 35.

34. Deed of December 15, 1910, between the Salvation Army and Thomas Day, Deeds Book 117, p. 235; deed of February 26, 1910, between the Salvation Army and Lucy Hidalgo and three children, Deeds Book 127, p. 156–57; deed of May 25, 1911, between the Salvation Army and Allen L. Roddick, Deeds Book 119, p. 234; deed of September 7, 1911, between the Salvation Army and Amy Porter, Deeds Book 129, p. 104; deed of September 26, 1911, between the Salvation Army and Ede Harding, Deeds Book 122, p. 257; deed of September 28, 1910, between the Salvation Army and John Anderson, Deeds Book 117, pp. 125–26 (this did not clear for two years); deed of August 26, 1912, between the Salvation Army and Winfield J. Scott, Deeds Book 127, p. 9; deed of June 30, 1913, between the Salvation Army and Thomas Bryant, Deeds Book 131, p. 262; deed of October 10, 1914, between the Salvation Army and Samuel Handley, Deeds Book 136, p. 264; deed of January 6, 1916, between the Salvation Army and Catherine Baetschen, Deeds Book 142, p. 305; deed of September 26, 1917, between the Salvation Army and David W. Wiley, Deeds Book 152, p. 257, all Deeds Books in the Monterey County Courthouse; William Barker to Ferris, June 13, 1910; September 16, 1911; August 21 and 26, 1912, all in PDR Romie, SAA.

35. Deed of August 26, 1912, between the Salvation Army and Fred Evans, Deeds Book 127, p. 10; deed of December 27, 1912, between the Salvation Army and James E. Gallaway, Deeds Book 129, p. 106; deed of January 8, 1914, between the Salvation Army and Charles M. Barney, Deeds Book 133, p. 349; deed of January 22, 1914, between the Salvation Army and William A. Rothe, Deeds Book 133, p. 258; deed of October 2, 1915, between the Salvation Army and Harrison R. Hoopes, Deeds Book 140, pp. 200–201, all in Monterey County Courthouse; see also the accounts of William G. Boswell, Arioslo Carle, Charles N. Handley, C. H. Hume and Ari James in Colonization Cash Books, SAA.

36. Erikson to Ferris, May 26, 1903, PDR Romie, SAA.

37. Deed of August 13, 1912, between the Salvation Army and Carl Erickson, Deeds Book 87, p. 144; deed of October 26, 1915, between the Salvation Army and Carl Erickson, Deeds Book 87, p. 429; deed of June 3, 1920, between the Salvation Army and Carl Erickson, Deeds Book 113, p. 467, Prowers County Courthouse.

38. Deed of February 20, 1907, between the Salvation Army and A. J. Davy, Abstracts Book H, p. 757; deed of October 1, 1912, between A. J. Davy and Joseph S. McMurtry, Abstracts Book 64, p. 635, both in Guaranty Abstract Company, Lamar.

39. Deed of January 17, 1911, between the Salvation Army and R. P. Frewing, Deeds Book 113, p. 155, Prowers County Courthouse; Robert P. Frewing Account, Colonization Cash Books, SAA.

40. Louis H. Kephart Account, Colonization Cash Books, SAA; deed of September 8, 1919, between the Salvation Army and L. H. Kephart, Deeds Book 113, pp. 372–73; petition of February 19, 1920, the Salvation Army to the New York Supreme Court, Oil and Gas Lease and Miscellaneous Book 119, pp. 453–54, both in Prowers County Courthouse.

41. Joseph Hargreaves Account, Colonization Cash Books, SAA; Joseph H. Hargreaves Interview (January 30, 1934); deed of July 18, 1922, between the Salvation Army and Joseph H. Hargreaves, Deeds Book 156, p. 65, Prowers County Courthouse.

42. *Pueblo Chieftain*, May 25, 1959 and March 7, 1965. In 1910, Frank McGrath was listed as a druggist at Amity. U.S. Ms Census of Prowers County, Colorado, 1910.

43. Quit-claim deed of September 11, 1906, between the Salvation Army and the Holly and Swink Railway Company, Quit-Claim Deed Record Book 43, p. 470; deed of June 8, 1909, between the Salvation Army and the Atchison Topeka and Santa Fe Railroad Company, Deeds Book 56, p. 498; deed of July 28, 1909, between the Salvation Army and School District No. 27, Deeds Book 79, p. 572, all in Prowers County Courthouse; William S. Barker to Ferris, May 15, 1909, Amity Correspondence, SAA; *Holly Chieftain*, October 23, 1908.

44. Deed of February 21, 1906, between the Salvation Army and the Mission School District, Deeds Book 89, p. 285; deed of December 5, 1909, between A. L. Roddick, Trustee for the Mission School District and the Salvation Army, Deeds Book 111, p. 225, both in Monterey County Courthouse; Erikson to Ferris, July 29 and August 26, 1905; Jacob U. Romig to Ferris, February 9, 1906; Holland to Ferris, January 22, 1907, copy, all in PDR Romie, SAA.

45. Deed of February 19, 1913, between the Salvation Army and the Fort Romie Grange No. 358, Deeds Book 129, p. 297, Monterey County Courthouse.

46. Deed of September 12, 1914, between the Salvation Army and the Fort Romie Water Company, Deeds Book 136, p. 488; deed of December 30, 1919, between the Salvation Army and the Fort Romie Water Company, Deeds Book 169, pp. 251–52; deed of October 17, 1916, between the Salvation Army and the Mission Methodist Episcopal Church, Deeds Book 146-D, p. 376, all in Monterey County Courthouse.

47. Quit-Claim Deed of January 26, 1922, between the Salvation Army (of New York) and the Salvation Army (of California), Quit-Claim Deeds Book 103, p. 452, Monterey County Courthouse.

48. This typical expression is from the deed of September 23, 1903, between the Salvation Army and Mathias Mathiesen, Deeds Book 75, pp. 403–4, Monterey County Courthouse. It is interesting to note that the same kind of clause forbidding the sale of liquor under penalty of reversion was in the deeds of California colonists at Long Beach and Ontario earlier. Gilman M. Ostrander, *The Prohibtion Movement in California, 1858–1933* (Berkeley and Los Angeles: University of California Press, 1957), p. 69.

49. Erikson, "The Fort Romie Contract," January 22, 1934, typescript, PDR Romie, SAA.

50. Subordination Agreement of March 8, 1934, signed by William C. Arnold and George Darby for the Salvation Army, copy; George Darby to Gene Pappani, November 1, 1939, copy, both in PDR Romie, SAA.

CHAPTER NINE: ALL THE WORLD A BATTLEFIELD

1. H. Rider Haggard to Theodore Roosevelt, June 13, 1905, "private," Roosevelt Papers, microfilm, Series 1, Reel 55.

2. *The War Cry* (NY), October 3, 1903; Shaw, "A Successful Farm Colony," p. 562.

3. *The War Cry* (NY), November 25, 1904.

4. Colonization Board Minutes, September 8, 1898, SAA; Booth-Tucker, "The Relation of Colonization to Irrigation," p. 503.

5. Booth-Tucker, "The Relation of Colonization to Irrigation," p. 500; Frederick Booth-Tucker, "Colonization," *Forestry and Irrigation* 9 (February 1903):86.

6. Frederick Booth-Tucker, "Colonization," *Foresty and Irrigation* 9 (February 1903):88.

7. Entry for September 16, 1903, Diary of Frederick Booth-Tucker, SAA; Emma Booth-Tucker to William Booth, September 22, 1903, National Commander Collection, SAA.

8. Booth-Tucker, "The Relation of Colonization to Irrigation," pp. 481, 502.

9. *Ibid.*, pp. 502−3, 503−4.

10. Entry for September 16, 1903, Diary of Frederick Booth-Tucker, SAA; Emma Booth-Tucker to William Booth, September 22, 1903, National Commander Collection, SAA.

11. *Ibid.*; *Denver Republican*, October 24, 1903; *The Irrigation Age* 19 (May, 1904):214.

12. *New York Times*, February 22, 1904.

13. *The Irrigation Age* 19 (May, 1904):214; *All the World* 26 (July, 1905): 354; *Congressional Record*, 58th Congress, 2nd Session (March 21, 1904), vol. 38, pt. 4:3454−55.

14. *Denver Republican*, October 25, 1903.

15. *The War Cry* (NY), May 14, 1904; *The Technical World* 2 (October, 1904):185−86; *The Irrigation Age* 19 (May, 1904); 214; *Field and Farm* 19 (March 5, 1904): 6; *New York Times*, March 21, 1904; *The Topeka Daily Capital*, March 22, 1904; *The Topeka State Journal*, March 22, 1904.

16. Frederick Booth-Tucker, "The Landless Man to the Manless Land," *The Technical World* 2 (October, 1904):189.

17. *Ibid.*, pp. 191−92.

18. Quoted in H. Rider Haggard, *The Days of My Life* (London: Longmans, Green & Co., Ltd, 1926), vol. 2, p. 73.

19. Alfred Lyttelton to Haggard, January 14, 1905, quoted in Haggard, *The Days of My Life*, pp. 173−74.

20. Lilias Rider Haggard, *The Cloak That I Left* (London: Hodder & Stoughton, 1951), p. 187.

21. Fred Graham to Haggard, January 31, 1905, in Haggard, *The Poor and the Land*, p. xxxix.

22. Albert Grey to Haggard, February 8, 1905, H. Rider Haggard MSS, University of California at Los Angeles Library.

23. Rudyard Kipling to Haggard, January 31, 1905, quoted in Morton Cohen, *Rider Haggard* (London, Melbourne & Toronto: Macmillan & Co., 1968), p. 59.

24. Frederick Russell Burnham to Haggard, February 15, 1905, H. Rider Haggard MSS, Henry E. Huntington Library, San Marino; Lilias Haggard, *The Cloak That I Left*, p. 188.

25. *The War Cry* (London), March 4, 1905; Haggard, *Days of My Life*, vol. 2, p. 176; Haggard, *The Poor and the Land*, pp. xl, 137−40.

26. Haggard, *The Poor and the Land*, pp. 28−30.

27. Haggard, *Days of My Life*, vol 2, pp. 177−78; Roosevelt to Haggard, March 11, 1905, Haggard MSS, Huntington Library.

28. Lilias Haggard, *The Cloak That I Left*, p. 188; Frederick Russell Burnham, *Scouting on Two Continents* (Garden City: Doubleday, Page & Co., 1927), 356; Haggard, *Days of My Life*, vol. 2, p. 191; *The War Cry* (London), April 8, 1905; London *Times*, April 28, 1905; Haggard, *The Poor and the Land*, p. 38.

29. Haggard, *The Poor and the Land*, p. 2; *The Autobiography of John Hays Hammond* (New York: Farrar & Rinehart, 1935), vol. 2, pp. 522−23; London *Times*, April 28, 1905.

30. *The War Cry* (London), March 25, 1905; *The War Cry* (NY), April 29, 1905; Denver *Times*, April 7, 1905; Haggard, *The Poor and the Land*, p. 67.

31. Haggard, *The Poor and the Land*, pp. 2, 3, 115−21; *All the World* 27 (April, 1906);179.

32. Haggard to Sir Wilfred Laurier, April 13, 1905; Laurier to Haggard, April 17, 1905, both in Haggard, *The Poor and the Land*, pp. 31, 36.

33. Arthur F. Sladen to Haggard, April 21, 1905, Haggard MSS, Huntington Library.

34. Booth-Tucker to Haggard, April 28, 1905, Haggard MSS, Huntington Library; Clifford Sifton to Haggard, April 16, 1905, quoted in Haggard, *The Poor and the Land*, p. 34.

35. Earl Grey to Haggard, May 20, 1905, Haggard MSS, Huntington Library.

36. Haggard to Roosevelt, June 13, 1905, "private," Roosevelt Papers, microfilm, Series 1, Reel 55; Roosevelt to Haggard, June 24, 1905, Haggard MSS, Huntington Library.

37. H. Rider Haggard, *Report on the Salvation Army Colonies in the United States and at Hadleigh, England, with Scheme of National Land Settlement*, House of Commons Sessional Papers (1905), vol. 53, pp. 2–5, 11–12, 22.

38. Haggard, *The Poor and the Land*, pp. vii, viii; Haggard, *Report*, 4.

39. *The War Cry* (London), June 24, July 1 and December 30, 1905; *All the World* 26 (August, 1905):401, 403; *The Times*, June 20, 1905.

40. July 3 and 24, 1905, *The Parliamentary Debates* 148:750; 150:38. Members of the Committee were: Lord Tennyson, Chairman; J. S. Davy, General Inspector of the Local Government Board; Arthur Wilson Fox, Deputy Comptroller General and Labour Commissioner, Board of Trade; Bernard Holland; Henry Lambert, Colonial Land Office; H. L. W. Lawson, Managing Committee of the Emigrants' Information Office; Colonel Lewellyn, Board of Agriculture; Herbert Samuel; and Sidney Webb. *Report of the Department Committee Appointed to Consider Mr. Rider Haggard's Report on Agricultural Settlements in British Colonies*, 1 House of Commons Sessional Papers (1906) vol. 76, p. 1.

41. Earl Grey to Haggard, July 4, 1905, quoted in Haggard, *Days of My Life*, vol. 2, p. 201.

42. Bramwell Booth to Haggard, August 3, 1906, quoted in Haggard, *Days of My Life*, pp. 201, 202.

43. *Ibid.*, p. 202.

44. *Report of the Department Committee*, pp. 5, 8.

45. *Ibid.*, pp. 9, 10–11, 20–21.

46. Haggard, *Days of My Life*, vol. 2, pp. 192, 195, 197; Morton Cohen, ed., *Rudyard Kipling to Rider Haggard* (London: Hutchinson & Co., Ltd., 1965), p. 72. For comments agreeing with the Committee, see *Mark Lane Express Agricultural Journal* 94 (June 25, 1906):711; 95 (July 23, 1906):98; C. C. Carstens, "The Salvation Army—A Criticism," *Annals of the American Academy of Political and Social Science* 30 (November, 1907):554–55.

47. Haggard, *Days of My Life*, vol. 2, p. 203.

48. Whitelaw Reid to Haggard, September 4, 1906, Haggard MSS, Huntington Library.

49. Haggard to *The Times*, March 14, 1907, draft; Haggard to Frederick R. Burnham, March 22, 1907, both in Haggard MSS, Huntington Library.

50. Booth-Tucker, "Farm Colonies" (1), pp. 988–89.

51. *New York Times*, November 25, 1903.

52. *New York Times*, November 30, 1906; *The Times*, February 22, 1907; Mrs. Roland Wilkins, "General Booth and the Land," p. 236.

53. Booth-Tucker, "Farm Colonies" (1), p. 989; *The Times*, August 1, 1905.

54. *The War Cry* (NY), July 21, 1906; Williams, *Booth-Tucker*, pp. 154, 172, 176–77, 188–89, 196; Frederick Booth-Tucker, *Muktifauj, or Forty Years With the Salvation Army in India and Ceylon* (London: Salvationist Publishing & Supplies, 1923), pp. 163, 171–76, 203–40.

55. *All the World* 26 (February, 1905):60–61; *The War Cry* (London), April 22 and May 6, 1905; *New York Times*, April 27 and August 4, 1905.

56. *The War Cry* (London), December 16, 1905.

57. Elizabeth Hunter, "Transplanting a City's Poor," *World's Work* 14 (July, 1907):9153–54; Agnes C. Laut, "The Salvation Army and England's Unemployed," *Review of Reviews* 39 (January, 1909):74–76.

58. *The War Cry* (NY), October 19, 1904.

59. Booth-Tucker to Herbert Booth, February 17, 1902, copy, National Commander Collection, SAA.

60. *The War Cry* (SF), July 21, 1900; *The War Cry* (NY), October 29, 1904.

61. Booth-Tucker Testimony of October 3, 1905, *Minutes of Evidence* (1906), 76:33.

62. *New York Times*, October 30, 1903; *The War Cry* (NY), October 29, 1903.

63. Wisbey, *Soldiers Without Swords*, pp. 137–39; Williams, *Booth-Tucker*, pp. 165–69; *Social News* 1 (July, 1911):9.

64. Bolton Hall, *Three Acres and Liberty* (New York: Macmillan Co., 1918), pp. v, 1; Ralph Borsodi, *Flight From the City: An Experiment in Creative Living on the Land* (New York and London: Harper & Brothers, 1933), 189.

65. William E. Smythe, *The Conquest of Arid America* (New York and London: Macmillan Co., 1905), 330.

66. Henry S. Anderson, "The Little Landers' Land Colonies: A Unique Agricultural Experiment in California," *Agricultural History* 5 (October, 1931):139–50.

67. *The Homestead* 55 (June 2, 1910):6, 12.

68. *Sunset* 30 (February, 1913):210.

69. Paul Conkin, *Tomorrow a New World: The New Deal Community Program* (Ithaca: Cornell University Press, 1959), pp. 20–21, 23–24; Haviland H. Lund, "Redistribution of the Labor Now Employed in Producing War Supplies," *The American Economic Review*, Supplement 7 (March, 1917):239–40, 242, 243–44; *Relief of Distress Due to Unemployment: Hearings before the Committee on Labor on H.R. 11055, H.R. 11056, and H.R. 12097, 72d Congress, 1st Session (1932), pp. 75, 76, 77, 78–79, 81–82, 83–84.*

70. Conkin, *Tomorrow a New World*, pp. 44–48; Elwood Mead, *Helping Men Own Farms: A Practical Discussion of Government Aid to Land Settlement* (New York: Macmillan Co., 1920), pp. 1–2, 163, 198–99.

71. Russell Lord and Paul H. Johnstone, eds., *A Place on Earth: A Critical Appraisal of Subsistence Homesteads* (Washington: Bureau of Agricultural Economics, 1942), pp. 6, 7; Conkin, *Tomorrow a New World*, pp. 51–54; Peter A. Speek, *A Stake in the Land* (New York and London: Harper & Brothers, 1921), pp. 98–103, 106–7; Mead, *Helping Men Own Farms*, pp. 192–97. For a detailed argument in favor of veterans' farms, dedicated "To Those SOLDIERS, SAILORS AND MARINES Who Would Become FARMERS And Thereby Promote NATIONAL PROSPERITY AND SOCIAL PROGRESS," and written by the Assistant Secretary of the Federal Farm Loan Board, see James B. Morman, *The Place of Agriculture in Reconstruction: A Study of National Programs of Land Settlement* (New York: E. P. Dutton & Co., 1919).

72. Borsodi, *Flight From the City*; M. G. Kains, *Five Acres* (New York: Greenberg, 1935).

73. Russell Lord, "Back to the Farm," *Forum* 89 (February, 1933):97–98.

74. "Henry Ford's Shotgun Gardens," *Literary Digest* 110 (September 12, 1931):10.

75. Lord & Johnstone, *A Place on Earth*, pp. 12, 23.

76. Alvin Johnson, "Relief from Farm Relief," *Yale Review* 22, new series (September, 1932):52–65; Malcolm McDermott, "An Agricultural Army," *South Atlantic Quarterly* 31 (April, 1932):176–83; Lord and Johnstone, *A Place on Earth*, pp. 15–16; Conkin, *Tomorrow a New World*, pp. 25–27.

77. *Congressional Record* (July 14, 1932), 72d Congress, 1st Session, vol. 75, pt. 14, p. 15385.

78. Conkin, *Tomorrow a New World*, pp. 6–7, 36, 88–89; Lord and Johntone, *A Place on Earth*, p. 33.

Bibliographical Essay

FOR THE GENERAL HISTORY of the Salvation Army in America, two books are especially useful: Herbert A. Wisbey, Jr., *Soldiers Without Swords: A History of the Salvation Army in the United States* (New York: Macmillan Co., 1956), written originally as a doctoral dissertation at Columbia University; and Edward H. McKinley, *Marching to Glory: The History of The Salvation Army in the United States of America, 1880–1980* (San Francisco: Harper & Row, 1980), written by a Salvationist historian for the one-hundredth anniversary of the Army in this country. But these are general treatments, in which discussion of the colonies is limited to a mere five pages in each, and at that more than in the broad multi-volumed, multi-authored official *The History of the Salvation Army* (London and New York: Thomas Nelson & Sons, 1947–1974, 6 vols.), begun by Robert Sandall.

Biographies of the leading figures of the farm colonization movement should include St. John Ervine, *God's Soldier: General William Booth* (1935), 2 vols., and the more official Harold Begbie, *Life of William Booth* (London: Macmillan & Co., 1920); Frederick Arthur Mackenzie, *Booth-Tucker: Sadhu and Saint* (London: Hodder & Stoughton, 1930) and the more up-to-date Harry Williams, *Booth-Tucker: William Booth's First Gentleman* (London, Sydney, Auckland, and Toronto: Hodder & Stoughton, 1980).

Essential for understanding the thinking behind the colonization movement is William Booth's classic statement, *In Darkest England and the Way Out* (London: The Salvation Army, 1890). Contemporary criticism of the General's ideas is summed up sketchily in Herman Ausubel, "General Booth's Scheme of Social Salvation," *American Historical Review* 56 (April 1951).

Indispensable in comprehending the American colonies are the articles and pamphlets by Frederick Booth-Tucker, especially *Prairie Homes For City Poor* (New York: no publisher, no date); *A Review of the Salvation Army Land Colony in California* (no place, no publisher, no date); *What Others Think of the Salvation Army Colony at Amity, Prowers County, Colorado* (no place, no publisher, 1904). "Farm Colonies of the Salvation Army," U.S. Bureau of Labor, *Bulletin* No. 48 (Washington, September 1903); "The Farm Colonies of the Salvation Army," *The Forum* 23 (August 1897); "Colonization and Irrigation," *Review of Reviews* 28 (November 1903); "The Relation of Colonization to Irrigation," *Forestry and Irrigation* 9 (October 1903); "Colonization," *Forestry and Irrigation* 9 (February 1903) and "The Landless Man to the Manless Land," *The Technical World* 2 (October, 1904).

Except for brief sketches in the popular periodical press, little has been written about Fort Romie in California. The same is true of Fort Herrick, but for an unpublished paper by Dorothy Hitzka, "Farm Colonies of the Salvation Army and in particular the Ft. Herrick Colony, Mentor, Ohio" (Cleveland: The Salvation Army Divisional Headquarters, March, 1976), which does not do full justice to the colony in a scholarly sense. More is available for Fort Amity in Colorado, including Albert Shaw, "A Successful Farm Colony in the Irrigation Country," *Review of Reviews* 26 (November 1902). Brief but well-balanced is Dorothy Roberts, "Fort Amity, the Salvation Army Colony in Colorado," *The Colorado Magazine* 17 (September 1940). A master's thesis at Kansas State Teachers College at Emporia, "The Amity Colony," by Marie Antalek (1968) is an excellent piece of work based primarily on newspapers and written prior to the opening of the Army's Archives in New York. Probably the best single source for all three colonies is H. Rider Haggard, *The Poor and the Land* (London and Bombay: Longmans, Green & Co., 1905), published after a visit for the purpose of eliciting British governmental support for overseas settlement.

Among the prime sources are the Salvation Army publications themselves, especially *The War Cry*, of which I have used the London edition in the British Museum and the New York and San Francisco editions in the United States. In addition, *All the World* (London), *The Conqueror* (New York), and *Harbor Lights* (New York) all contain considerable pertinent, but not disinterested, descriptions and commentaries.

A number of newspapers have been particularly fruitful. For Amity, the *Holly Chieftain*, the Denver *Republican*, and *The Rocky Mountain News* have been invaluable. Only a few broken runs of Salinas newspapers exist at the Bancroft Library and the Monterey County Library in Salinas and I have relied more on a variety of San Francisco papers. The London *Times*, the New York *Tribune*, and an assortment of Chicago newspapers have also been utilized.

Because of the importance of land titles and their transfer in the colonies, I have consulted courthouse records in Monterey County (Salinas), California, and Prowers County (Lamar), Colorado. In both instances, records of deeds, mortgages, contracts, lawsuits, and other legal matters have contributed a great deal to understanding of both agricultural and colonization problems. Abstracts of the Guaranty Abstract Company of Lamar, Colorado, were also of considerable value.

Now at the Houston Public Library, the valuable John Ephrain Thomas Milsaps Collection of personal diaries, scrapbooks of clippings, posters, pamphlets, and photographs was compiled by a veteran of Salvation Army work on the Pacific Coast and is a veritable treasure trove of material for almost any aspect of the Army's work in the West, the colonies not excepted. Two small collections of H. Rider Haggard papers have also been useful. Both stem from his 1905 visit to all three American colonies: one is at the Huntington Library; the other is housed at the University of California at Los Angeles.

But the real core of this study are the sources in the Salvation Army Archives and Research Center at 145 West 15th Street, New York City—records which detail the Army's overall colonization policy as well as the day-to-day problems, expenses and relationships of individual settlers. Some of the most important materials are included in the Finance Department records, especially Fort Romie Cash Book, October 1901–January 1910 (microfilm), Colonization Department Cash Ledger, October 1, 1901–September 30, 1910 (microfilm F44), Colonization Department Cash Books, October 16, 1901–September 29, 1910 (microfim, F132), and Finance Board and Council Minutes, 1894–1908 (AS-11). Several groups within the Property Department records are also rich in colony information: Romie Colony (RG # 2.6, 22-21-6); Records on Fort Romie (Ac. 82-76); Correspondence, Amity file (RG #2.6, 22-8-19); Fort Herrick Documents (Ac. 81-19); and Legal Secretary's Correspondence, 1901–1906 (AS-1).

In addition, other miscellaneous collections in the Archives have yielded significant information and insights, among them, the Richard E. Holz MSS, the Unprocessed National Commander Collection (Ac. 78-25), and several subcollections relating to colonization—Finance Ledger from Amity Colony, November 1899–December 1901 (Farm Colonies: MS 50-1-4), undated Cash Book (on Amity's first settlers) (Farm Colonies: MS 50-1-1) and Finance Ledger for Fort Herrick Colony, June 1898–October 1901 (Farm Colonies: M50-1-3). Also of great value are the Archive's printed collections, which range from splendid runs of almost all Salvation Army periodicals, to *Yearbooks*, histories, biographies, and annual financial statements.

Index